Susan Bennet
Martin R I

THE BODY OF 9

DECODE YOUR NATURAL PHYSIOLOGY
AND DISCOVER YOUR TRUE SELF

LIVE AN INSPIRED LIFE!

Susan Bennett Fisher
Martin R Fisher

THE BODY OF 9

DECODE YOUR NATURAL PHYSIOLOGY
AND DISCOVER YOUR TRUE SELF

LIVE AN INSPIRED LIFE!

Cover design by the Body of 9 Team
Illustrations by Branson Faustini, Katharine Cameron
Photos from Paolo Scoglio, Samantha Kok and Tonya Lessley

First edition: 2020

Printed in the United States of America

ISBN-13 978-1-7355655-0-7

Susan and Martin Fisher live in Bozeman, Montana. Find more information about opportunities for getting identified or learning to activate your Natural Number on Bodyof9.com/bookinfo

Dedication:

To our daughters for teaching us so much about life, the Natural Numbers, and the importance of presence in relationship.

Table of Contents

INTRODUCTION --1

THE CONTEXT: WHAT IS BODY OF 9?--2

WHAT ARE THE APPLICATIONS AND BENEFITS?------------------------------16

A SUMMATION OF FINDINGS--38

THE WORLD CONTEXT ---40

COMPARISON WITH PSYCHOLOGICAL MODELS-----------------------------42

READY TO FIND OUT ABOUT YOUR NATURAL NUMBER?------------------49

USERS' GUIDE TO THE 9 NATURAL NUMBERS -------------------------------50

NATURAL NUMBER 1 (NN1)--55

NATURAL NUMBER 2 (NN2)--79

NATURAL NUMBER 3 (NN3) --100

NATURAL NUMBER 4 (NN4) --126

NATURAL NUMBER 5 (NN5) --148

NATURAL NUMBER 6 (NN6) --174

NATURAL NUMBER 7 (NN7) --200

NATURAL NUMBER 8 (NN8) --231

NATURAL NUMBER 9 (NN9) --252

BEYOND IDENTIFICATION ---275

ABOUT THE TEAM--282

Introduction

Take a deep breath and unfasten your intellectual seat belt. You're about to be given a key to better understand who you really are, what shapes your view of the world and, most of all, why you think and act the way you do. It's an opportunity to unleash your full capacity to live a more inspired life.

What we've all been missing is a method to unlock, turn-on, and drive our personal operating systems. The Body of 9 offers a comprehensive, body-based process to better understand ourselves. We're continually informed by our physical bodies through the nine distinct regions in the body that directly impact the way we experience our lives. We're each born with one region that's activated at birth. This active region is what we call our Natural Number (NN).

Based on that active region, the body develops and presents distinct physical characteristics, specifically in posture, movement, and structure, using specific muscles, bones, and fascia. These innate physical characteristics, which are governed by nature rather than nurture, directly determine how we relate to ourselves and to others.

Knowing this key exists, wouldn't you want to verify your essential identity and use it to amplify and project your truest and best self? If the answer is yes, then let's get rolling to decipher your Natural Number. Once we've defined it, you'll be able to recognize the origins and patterns of your physical, mental, and emotional behaviors. With this Natural Number awareness, you'll have a new and improved ability to acknowledge and appreciate your fundamental thinking, actions, and reactions, and best utilize the intrinsic gifts you've been given to share.

As we move into the specifics of this game-changing personal examination, just envision that by the time you get to the end of this book, you'll be embracing this deeper understanding of self. This work is about the YOU and the MORE that you've always wanted to know, and offers you an extraordinary opportunity to live a life of greater freedom, clarity and purpose. And yes: it's right there waiting for you.

Get ready to embark on the game-changing journey to your truest and best self.

The Context: What is Body of 9?

Our bodies have an even greater impact on our existence than most of us can imagine. Without the knowledge of how our bodies impact our reality, our wisdom and gifts go unnoticed and unappreciated and get lost in the messiness of our human experience.

This book introduces the discovery of a human context, based in our bodies. Understanding this context allows us to know ourselves better, be happier, have healthier, more enjoyable relationships, and – most importantly – to make sense of ourselves within the context of all that is. This gives you the freedom to have the impact and live the purpose you are here to embody.

The Body of 9 is a handbook for learning to use our bodies' natural capabilities to improve our senses, our tools, our gifts, and our skills. Furthermore, it teaches how these strengths vary from those of others in our lives. This book seeks to empower you to be your best self – proud, acknowledged, and unafraid – while supporting those in your life to do the same.

It Starts with You

Over the course of your life, you may have had moments of awareness, epiphany, or realization that went beyond what you could rationalize – or for that matter, describe – yet felt profoundly true, and indeed proved true time and again. You may have had a sense that there is much more to that awareness than you understood, much more to yourself. But what is that "more", and how can you understand it?

There is an old allegory about three people who were blindfolded and placed touching part of an elephant. They were asked to describe the object they were touching. One, at the tail said, "It is long and thin, with hair at the ends. It is like a broom or a whip." The one placed at a foot of the elephant said, "It is solid, round, rough on the outside, and I cannot move it from the ground; it must be some sort of tree trunk." The third, holding onto the ear, exclaimed, "It is wide, thin, and it flaps back and forth, moving the air – it must be some sort of fan." While none of them were wrong in their observations, none could sense that they only had one part of a larger creature. Without the context of the whole, the information they were receiving, while accurate, didn't help them understand what was actually in front of them – an elephant.

In this case, each of us is the elephant, and each of us is only experiencing a part of ourselves and others. Though we understand parts of ourselves, we often miss the greater sum, and often only look at ourselves from one vantage point. Even knowing that we are only aware of part of the elephant, when we struggle with confusion, sadness, worry, stress, or trauma, realizing that there is more at play than we understand can add to our discomfort. The full picture feels beyond our grasp.

Yet that full picture is still *your*; it is your own wholeness that informs it. Learning to access that wholeness, rather than just a few component parts, is the key to the "more" that you know is there. This book is about how to use your body to actively find that wholeness – that "more" you've sensed – and use it with consciousness and choice.

The Body of 9 presents a new context for your personal experience that will help you make sense of the world. It describes the physical ability that you already possess and teaches you how to actively manifest and enhance this strength and power. It is about describing the whole elephant, such that each of us can leap into the unknowns of life, unconstrained and unafraid, to explore the possibility offered to us in, through, and beyond, our bodies.

9 Bodies, 9 Physical Regions

After extensive study spanning people of many ages, ethnicities, and cultures, the context presented in Body of 9 submits a simple observation: there are more than seven billion people in the world, but only nine physiologically different presentations: nine kinds of bodies.

The human body has nine regions of activation; only one is naturally active at birth, which we refer to as your Natural Number. Each person then grows through different life experiences, which shape their reality and determine the "nurture" influences of their life. How they process these experiences, however, and how they engage with the world is directly and intimately connected to their primary physiology described by their Natural Number.

Each Natural Number has a region of the body that is comprised of a set of muscles, bones, and fascia. When activated through posture, attention, and intention, a shift occurs in our processing that affects how the primary senses are decoded, and allows access to other physical and nonphysical information sources. This provides different information and perspective to a person, depending on which region is activated.

However, as mentioned earlier, only one of those nine regions is born active in each person. This results in different parts of the body being developed in particular ways depending on the active region, effectively creating nine physiologically different kinds of people. Though one can learn to activate the other regions, it is the original Natural Number region that influences a person's core investment in reality; as such, two people of different Natural Numbers have vastly different methods of experiencing and engaging with the world, both of which are entirely valid and valuable, yet alien to the other. This can be the crux of great conflict, but also great strength; this book will equip you with the understanding to tap that strength.

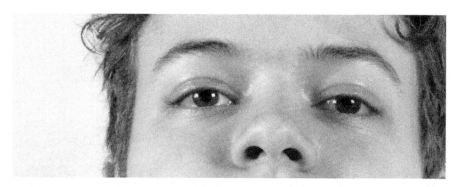

Natural Number 1

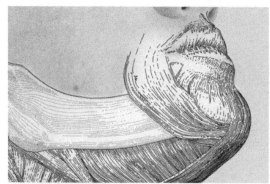

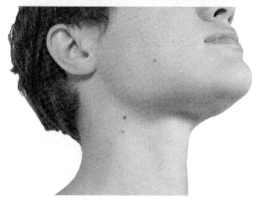

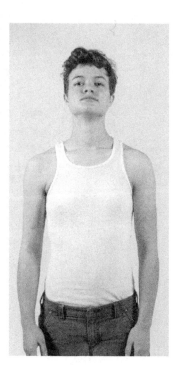

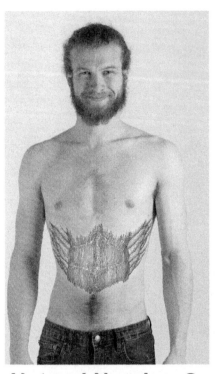
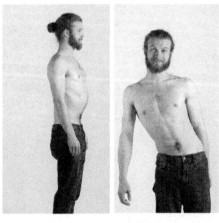
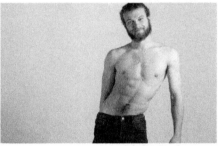

Natural Number 2

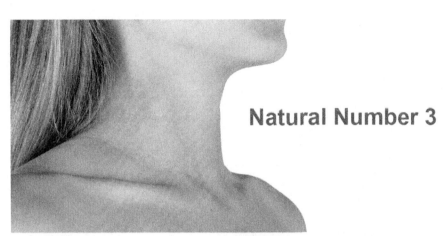

Natural Number 3

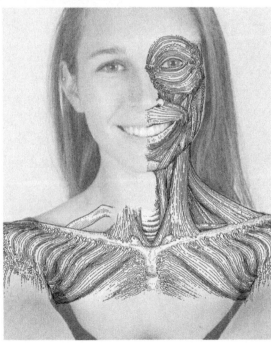

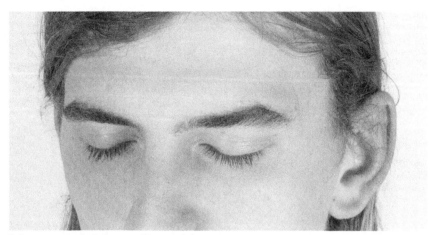

Natural Number 4

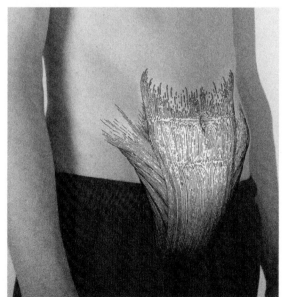

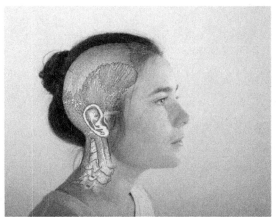

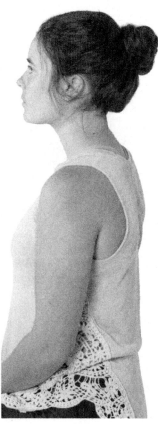

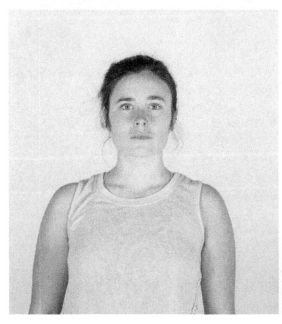

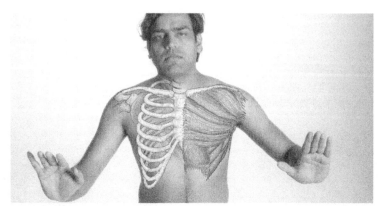

Natural Number 6

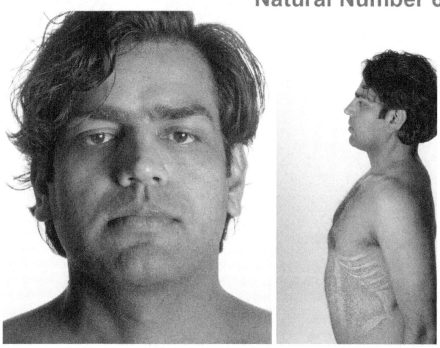

Natural Number 7

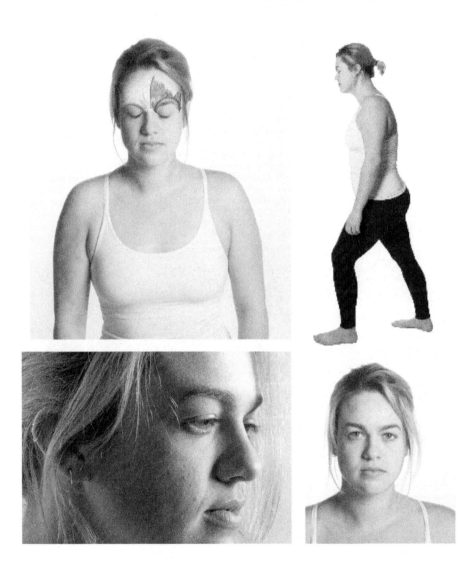

11

Natural NUMBER 8

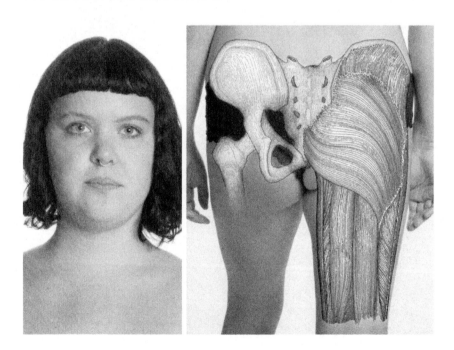

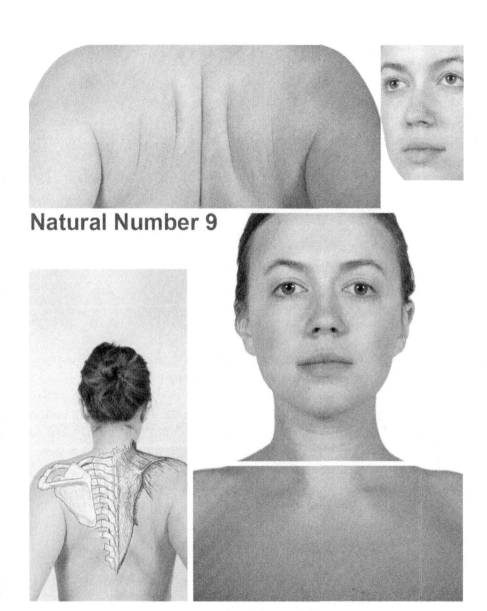

Natural Number 9

How Do We Identify a Person's Natural Number?

We watch for very specific physical and energetic markers when identifying a person's Natural Number. We look at things such as eye quality, body structure, muscular tension in the face, and other such markers. We look for consistency and preponderance of characteristics; finally, we look for a person to resonate powerfully with the Natural Number's description, and be satisfied with the identification experience.

- Body Structure: The musculature of our face, head, chest, and lower body develop differently depending on which region of the body is most active. There are physiological markers specific to each Natural Number, some combination of which must be present in order to confirm a person's Natural Number.

- Movement: Each activated region is comprised of a specific grouping of local muscles, bones, and associated soft tissue. This is the 'driving force' of where movement is initiated and centred in each person. It influences the style and manner in which our bodies move – how we lift, bend, and rotate are all related to our Natural Number's region. Gestures and physical performance all initiate in, and are centred around, the region related to our Natural Number. Specific types of movement support the activation of each Natural Number's region.

- Facial Expression: When activated, people of each Natural Number display a distinct facial expression, including particular sequences of micro-movements and eye quality. The shape, muscular hold, and movement of the jaw, cheeks, and mouth are key elements of these expressions.[1] In addition, face shape is often distinct to each Natural Number. These similarities tend to be consistent across ethnicities, but there are some variations, depending on genetic and racial characteristics, that a facilitator must learn to accommodate.

---

[1] The Facial Expressions of Activation, naturally occurring phenomena in the human body, were first noticed by New Equations ®. The details and components of the facial expressions have since been refined through research by Body of 9 leaders Susan and Martin Fisher

- Posture: Each Natural Number has a primary physical posture that facilitates activation, and can be used to identify which region is most active in a person. Physical exercises are available at the end of each Natural Number specific chapter to help you understand the different postures.

- Energy Signature: Each Natural Number, when stimulated in the body, has a particular energetic impact or signature that others can feel. During the identification process, the activation creates a state change in the body for the facilitator, the participant being identified, and even the observers. The participant generally becomes relaxed and comfortable, or in some cases exhilarated, with the experience. The sensation of being seen and honoured at a deep level, sometimes as never before, is profoundly affirming. Beyond identification, the energetic signature can be observed and experienced by noticing how we interact with and carry ourselves around others. The change is most clear when we present our most authentic, empowered selves.

The particular manifestation of each of these markers for each Natural Number will be described in later, Natural Number specific chapters.

What happens when a person is disabled or injured?

Injury, trauma, makeup, plastic surgery, disabilities, and pain can all obscure the physiological markers, impact movement, and affect a person's ability to hold a posture or fully activate a center. It is important to account for the current physical state of a person being identified, as well as any significant and relevant history. For example, if a person is blind, but has Natural Number 1, 2, 3, or 4, where eye contact is part of the activation, you can still identify their Natural Number. It may be more challenging to identify and to provide a powerful experience for them. However, having a disability that affects your ability to access your Natural Number often leads to the enhancement of other aspects of the characteristics and abilities that come with the Natural Number. For example, a blind Natural Number 4 might develop their ability to more easily go inside and create a deeper connection through the low abdomen, or they might use touch when not having eye contact available as a way of creating intimacy in the connection.

What are the Applications and Benefits?

In Personal Growth and Development

The context provided by the Body of 9 makes a difference in knowing who you are, what innate strengths you possess and how you can easily access them to have a more fulfilling life. Experiencing your body's natural way of being is an acknowledgement of the amazing human you are. When you understand, honour, and support your core self, your greater self is invited into action. You become more efficient, clear, and impactful. There is a comfort of being in your own skin that leads to greater joy and confidence. Your purpose – and the possibility of pursuing that purpose – becomes more available.

In the Real World: Maria

In her early forties, Maria – recently divorced, her son grown and married, dissatisfied with her accounting career, and scared but wanting to explore living somewhere new – began searching. She knew that more was available, and that she had a much bigger purpose. She started researching, and began her transformation process with Landmark. Through Landmark, she learned how to take personal responsibility. Then a friend brought her to a Body of 9 event where she was Identified as a Natural Number 8. At first, she was resistant to this new information about her body, but as she explored her power and learned more about what being a Natural Number 8 meant, everything began to fall into place. Today, four years later, she is CFO at a large Community Foundation in the city of her choice, and is in a stable long-term relationship – living that "more" she knew was possible. She attributes much of her transition to more deeply understanding her strengths skills and gifts that come with her Natural Number 8.

In Relationships

Recognizing that the people around us have different bodies informing their experience of reality provides new insight. Understanding the differences in how we interact, what we care about, and what we offer enables us to empathize and thrive with the various members of our communities. It deepens relationships by improving communication, engagement, and connection; it enables us to honour and appreciate others on a profound level.

By applying this context, couples can restore the initial attraction, wonder, and awe that heralds the beginning of the relationship while fortifying the love that develops over time. Friends estranged by misunderstanding can meet each other with greater openness and empathy by refraining from self-informed judgments. The appreciation of a loved one can become lost amidst the conflicts and stressors that create cracks in the connection; rather than trying to change the fundamental attributes of your partner, you can learn to respect, honour, and support them. They, in turn, can do the same for you.

In the Real World: Paolo Scoglio, Relationship Coach

Paolo is a psychotherapist, trained coach, and certified Body of 9 Facilitator. He was working with a couple that was having relationship challenges, and had lost the connection to their original love for each other. Paolo identified the couple, explaining the unique ways they communicated and the special skills and gifts that came with their Natural Numbers. The exercises he did with the couple reconnected them to what they had fallen in love with at the start of their relationship. It taught them the differences in their communication styles – one needed eye contact to feel seen and heard, where eye contact was distracting to the other. One needed time alone to recharge, and the other needed close connection. Knowing these needs and ways of being were built into their bodies rather than willful withholdings or recalcitrance on the part of their partner created understanding and acceptance. It enabled them to honour and respect what their partner needed, avoiding disappointment and promoting a deeper and more loving relationship. After years of bickering over small issues the chipped away at the core of the relationship, they began to rebuild and reconnect to the beauty and uniqueness they offered to each other.

In Family

Family relationships are among the most complicated that we face. We have not chosen these relationships; they come to us by virtue of our birth. The Body of 9 explains the complications we encounter in our families, the why and how of when we are not supported, and conversely, when we fail to support others. It improves parenting by offering ideas and strategies for nurturing the different needs of each child, helping children emerge as adults with greater assuredness and understanding for who they are. It changes sibling relationships from competitive, combative, or confusing to appreciative, accepting, and honouring, even in disagreement. Introducing the context of the Body of 9 in the family is extraordinarily powerful for healing and fortifying the group as a whole.

In the Real World: Nancy

Nancy, Natural Number 3, has two daughters; the older one is a Natural Number 5 and the younger one is a Natural Number 7. Her husband has Natural Number 2. In this case, both parents build relationships through eye contact, and both kids are actually distracted by eye contact when conversing or trying to answer questions. After learning about this difference, Nancy and her husband stopped demanding that their kids look them in the eye when they were talking to them. This has created much more harmony in the family.

In the situation where the older sibling has Natural Number 5 and the younger has Natural Number 7, some common problems occur. When told no after making a request, the Natural Number 5 will generally accept the answer. She will not push to get her way. Rather, she will understand that there was a reason for her parent's decision, and as long as it has been explained to her, she will accept the ruling.

However, her younger sister, the Natural Number 7, constantly pushes the boundaries of any decision, and has all sorts of ideas of ways around the "no" that she has received. This means that Nancy and her husband often end up giving in to the request eventually, after growing exhausted trying to resist. The Natural Number 5 sees this as inconsistent and unfair.

If this is not addressed in how they are parented, it can lead to the Natural Number 5 developing resentment toward her sister and her parents. After this dynamic was understood more clearly from the standpoint that these behaviours are attributes of their bodies, not aberrations in their character, Nancy and her husband were able to develop different ways to support each child. By giving the Natural Number 7 free reign to explore possibility and boundaries while still honouring the fairness and congruity needed by their older Natural Number 5 child, they created more harmony in the kids' relationship.

In the Workplace

In the workplace we encounter yet more adversity. For the most part, we have not chosen our colleagues, and suddenly there is hierarchy, there is risk, there is a pressing fear of loss and failure. This translates into a catalyst for emotional trauma, stress, and illness. This is not, however, an unavoidable reality of the workplace. The context provided by the Body of 9 builds the foundation for a supportive environment.

On the personal level, it teaches physical ways of recovering when under stress. On a larger scale, it provides an understanding of the skills and strengths each team member brings to the table. It offers explanations for the often bewildering behaviour of others, and promotes acceptance, authenticity, and safety among colleagues. When people feel valued and honoured for their contribution – when they know how and why they are important to the whole process – they become more effective and efficient. Teams go from complexity to clarity, from conflict to coherence.

When teams are put together consciously to include all nine Natural Numbers, they are balanced, inclusive, and highly effective. Non-hierarchical teams with all nine valued equally and invited equally to contribute produce solutions that are receivable and understandable by more customers. Once your organization understands that there are nine vastly different approaches, each of which has value and applicability to every situation, you can begin to develop solutions that are more universal, or more specifically targeted depending on what you are trying to accomplish.

In the Real World: Our Organization

At Body of 9, rather using a hierarchical structure, we use the understanding of our Natural Numbers and the organizational structure of geese flying in formation:[2]

- When the lead goose tires, it rotates back into the formation and another goose flies to the point position. Different team members take the lead at different times so no one person carries the full burden — you lead when your skills and gifts are most needed.

- As each goose flaps its wings it creates an "uplift" for the birds that follow. By flying in a "V" formation, the whole flock adds 71% greater flying range than if each bird flew alone. Teams that share the work go faster and further with greater ease. Each Natural Number needs the skills and gifts offered by the others in order for their gift to have context to be useful and on-point. The input from the others makes your contribution more valuable.

- The geese flying in formation honk to encourage those up front to keep up their speed. Encouragement and support is critical to all performing challenging roles. Natural Numbers 1 through 4 help the group to understand that connection and support are an important ingredient of success; they show all the others how to encourage, recognize, and support all members of the group. Natural Numbers 5 through 9 must each play their transformational part to create success

---

[2] Adapted from "LESSONS FROM GEESE" by Milton Olson, adapted by Angeles Arrien

for the overall project. Each Natural Number enhances and supports the others.

- When a goose gets sick, wounded, or shot down, two geese drop out of formation and follow it down to help and protect it. They stay with it until it dies or is able to fly again. Then, they launch out with another formation or catch up with the flock. When we stand by each other in difficult times as well as when we are strong, the community grows stronger. No one is left on their own. This eliminates fear, and creates a sense of connection and aligned commitment, making a more productive and happy working community.

At Body of 9, wherever possible, all nine Natural Numbers are included. Any significant product design, important decision, or marketing message is reviewed by at least one person of each Natural Number. For example, this book was read, edited, and reviewed by at least one person of each Natural Number before it was published.

In Performance

Understanding how movement is initiated in the body can dramatically improve physical performance – speed, endurance, and execution of physical activities can be enhanced through understanding which region of the body is naturally activated. When the Natural Number region is consciously activated and used during performance, be it sports, dance, or any physical activity, the activity is more easily and effortlessly executed. When you see a truly beautiful performance, be it music, dance, theatre, or film, when there is authenticity to the performance, the performer is usually finding a way to access the power of their Natural Number. When we are aligned with ourselves in performance, it can be very attractive, engaging, and believable.

In the Real World: Natural Numbers in Performance

Michael Jordan, a professional basketball player, is a Natural Number 3; we were able to identify him through his movement, body structure, and facial expression. He used the activation of his upper-sternum, lifting from the manubrium, to seemingly float through the air. His ability to hold the ball using long, straight arms – directly out from his shoulders – extended his reach, and his tremendous focus enabled him to come through in clutch moments when everything but his intention was blocked out. These are all features of Natural Number 3. He also used his incredible Natural Number 3 ability to inspire and lead his team to greatness, and simultaneously garner the hearts of his fan base. Jordan used the unique combination of his Natural Number skills and gifts to achieve success that was amazing to others.

Similarly, when you watch a gold medal performance in the Olympics, you are seeing people who have both practiced until their performance is embodied, but they are also finding a way to access the power and strength of their Natural Number. When one athlete all the sudden reaches another level of performance, the activation of the Natural Number is almost always involved. When you see an athlete crumble under pressure, they have lost their connection to their innate power and strength in their body. This is why posture and attitude are talked about so extensively in performance. Our bodies naturally activate when our posture supports the activation of our Natural Number. When skill and conditioning are equal, – winning comes down to the person who can hold onto their concentration, focus, and strength – conscious activation of your Natural Number's region enables you to do this.

Acting and casting for television and film is another practical application for understanding and applying the Natural Number activations. This is particularly applicable when casting for a person who ages significantly over the course of a television show, or when there are flashbacks to them in their youth. People cast as the same character at different ages are most believable when they share a Natural Number.

In biographical stories, when the Natural Number of the actor is matched to that of the real person, you get much more natural portrayals of character and movement. For example, there were two films about Steve

22

Jobs, Natural Number 7. One featured Ashton Kutcher, also Natural Number 7 – that movie had a greater factor of accuracy and authenticity. The following film about Steve Jobs featured Michael Fassbender, Natural Number 3. Fassbender was not able to bring in the innate vulnerability of Natural Number 7, making his portrayal of Steve Jobs hard and unyielding.

An actor is much more likely to win acclaim for their portrayal of a character when they share Natural Number with the person they are playing. For example, Reese Witherspoon played June Carter, both Natural Number 1; Ramey Malek played Freddie Mercury, both Natural Number 1; Meryl Streep played Margaret Thatcher, both Natural Number 8. All of these performances were praised for the actor's ability to capture the essence of the person they were playing.

How will Learning your Natural Number Change your Life?

Having your Natural Number identified is an affirming experience that contributes to a process of growth. If you liken it to cultivating a tree, the identification process is akin to planting the acorn. The seed has been introduced to an environment that will allow it to begin sprouting roots, and transition into a new state of existence. A great deal of work and support lie ahead before it becomes a fully formed oak tree; the acorn will require water, nutrients, sunlight, and safety to grow, but the journey has begun. The roots systems will become more robust and complex, and a sapling with soon break the surface to change the landscape above.

When you have your Natural Number identified, a seed of understanding is planted in your being that will continue to grow on its own. Knowing your Natural Number can instill or restore a sense of stability and logic to your life. We see people become more content and aligned with their values and sense of purpose following their first intentional activation.

Once you have a conscious awareness of your Natural Number, your relationship with yourself will begin to shift. The core aspects of your strengths and perceptions come forward; some describe this as "your soul taking the lead". We also describe it as activating your neutral Observer.

This enables you to look at your beliefs and behaviors from a new vantage point in order to make more informed decisions regarding your identity. This is one of the primary benefits of knowing your Natural Number.

Another major benefit is expanding your capacity to learn. Your body-based ability to absorb information will sharpen, as will your comprehension and synthesis of that information. New perceptions, potentials, connections, and transformations become possible.

The identification process is a unique experience for everyone. When the power within you is first awakened, so too is the feeling of assuredness in this reality. It is a novel and validating physical awareness of your natural power and capabilities.

Just as a gardener must be attentive to their plants to nurture them into full bloom, so too can a person nurture the development of their conscious access to the skills, values, and strengths of their Natural Number.

The more you cultivate your connection to your Natural Number, the stronger and more accessible it will become. Doing so provides:

- a simple physical process that lets you connect back to your core being

- a body-based ability to recover when you are triggered with emotions that take you to an un-present state

- a new understanding of what it means for you to be present

- the ability to activate your conscious neutral Observer – to view your actions from a non-attached perspective

In addition, using the skills and strength of your Natural Number enables you:

- to see, understand, and consciously choose your behaviours

- to learn the pitfalls of attributing motive to the behaviours of others based solely on your perspective

- to understand that eight out of nine other people do not 1) experience life the way you do, 2) perceive what you perceive, 3) understand what is obvious to you, or 4) care about that which you consider essential, and to recognize that the reverse is also true

When understood this can create a new level of compassion and possibility for communication. We can stop making up what we think other people mean, and use curiosity to begin to explore others' intent and thinking.

All of this translates to better, deeper relationships, matched with a more profound acceptance of yourself and how your body informs your life experiences. As your understanding of yourself and others undergoes this metamorphosis, you are empowered to approach the complexity of life with confidence in your value, and the value of those around you.

Once your primary Natural Number has been identified, introspection will follow, examining and comprehending the wholeness of your being. You can then learn how to use your body to activate your primary Natural Number consciously, using the muscles, bones, and soft tissue that already function as sensors for the bulk of your experience.

Each Natural Number (NN), when active, offers something entirely different from the others. Here are the core benefits for learning each of the Natural Numbers:

1. NN1 honours others and treats them with respect, holding all equally, and providing each person with a sense of value.

2. NN2 engages with another person as they exist in the moment, without agenda.

3. NN3 experiences the intense joy and energy of togetherness at the pure soul-level of connection.

4. NN4 offers insight into self, in order to align with your core being and with others for more intimate, authentic connection.

5. NN5 helps others to achieve their purpose, calms the mind, and reveals congruity between information and its source, whether to confirm or challenge its validity.

6. NN6 senses when and how to generate energy to move a group, project, or person into action, knowing what must follow to align with the greatest good for all involved.

7. NN7 effectively instigates change, opens minds to new possibilities, and optimizes the efficiency of these new potentials and processes.

8. NN8 uses the body to develop trust and shape integrity in ways that create safety for all. It grounds the creative process in realistic tasks and actions for different members of a group.

9. NN9 helps you know your place in the Universal flow, so that you can create efficiently with harmony and balance, without using excess energy or force to bring coherence.

Introduction to the Authors

Susan Bennett Fisher, with assistance from her husband and business partner, Martin R. Fisher, has consolidated, synthesized and presented the research and learning accumulated over the last 9 years of experimentation and study. Importantly, this book also derives from the work, contributions, and wisdom of our colleagues, teachers, students, families, and all the people who have had their Natural Number identified. This book brings together all the voices, perspectives, and wisdom of the Body of 9 as they function individually and together. We are grateful to all who have contributed to building the context of this powerful understanding.

Susan, Natural Number 6, was initially introduced to the concept of the 9 Natural Numbers in 2002 by New Equations[3], as part of a leadership

---

[3] New Equations is the organization that first identified and categorized the nine physiologically

training program offered by The Coaches Training Institute, CTI. The identification experience was so profound that she knew she had found her calling – to be the messenger for this work to the world. She has since dedicated herself to understanding, researching, and educating others about the Body of 9.

Martin, Natural Number 5, moved from England, where he was born and raised, to Silicon Valley in 1981. Susan identified his Natural Number in 2007, and he immediately saw the value of this knowledge as it helped make everything existing in his framework become more congruent.

There is more information available on Susan, Martin, and the history of their work later in this book. Their experiences and learnings are also sprinkled throughout to help you understand how their work has shaped their understanding of themselves, each other, and the Body of 9.

Introduction to Susan Bennett Fisher: – The Start of her Story.

"I have a theory about human growth and spiritual development that is based on the work of a lifetime of exploring the "more" that is out there. We come into this world as spirit, we occupy a body, then we spend the next 28 years unlearning that which we came in with at the start. But if you look at a baby – it is hard to dispute the purity of spirit they embody. And yet we do.

When I was twelve, I had my first cosmic experience. I had fought with my younger sister over who got to sit where to watch our favourite television show. I got so mad that I punched my sister in the arm, pretty much as hard as I could. It was a bit foolish, as my mother was sitting there too, and she promptly sent me to my room. Steaming mad still, I opened my window and crawled out onto the ledge. It was a truly wondrous star-filled night. As I sat there, communing with the Universe, with all of the cosmos stretched out before me, a voice started to communicate with me. It told me that I was very powerful and had a great purpose, but that I would need to learn to direct the power of my energy for good; that I should never lose control and use that level of force against others as I came into my power.

different kinds of people.

I never told anyone about this experience – instead, I held it as a guide for my actions going forward. It was an intensely personal and powerful experience of the "more" that is out there. I stored it away, along with the knowing of how magical our existence could be.

I didn't choose to believe, and I didn't choose to disbelieve – I accepted the experience as a knowing that came with my version of existence. If I had known my Natural Number at the time, this experience would have made more sense, and I would probably have explored more openly as time went on. But I didn't know. I had no context for this experience, so while formative, it was not until many years later that I understood what I had done to create it."

The Research and Understanding

Introducing new information to the human community can be challenging. The most common objections we encounter to the assertion that there are nine physiologically different kinds of people are, "Why hasn't this been seen before?" and, "What is the scientific proof?" There is also an underlying question related to our findings: "How is it that you are presenting something that thousands of scientists, doctors, and psychologists don't know?"

The lack of awareness surrounding a phenomenon, or the inability to measure it, is a misleading rule to use in disproving its presence. The existence of electromagnetic waves wasn't formally hypothesized until 1873; they weren't actually detected until 1895. Of course, such waves existed prior to 1873; we simply lacked the tools to observe them, much less the notion to look for such a thing.

Similarly, we believe our process and research will eventually lead to the 9 Natural Numbers being as commonly accepted as electromagnetic waves. We are working diligently to develop the required underlying research and methods to demonstrate proof, and progress is being made.

Both Susan and Martin Fisher are educated in classic disciplines. Susan Studied Mathematical Economics and Computer Science at Brown University. This education taught her about the rigors of research and analysis. She also obtained her MBA in Finance and Management and a Masters in International Business as a fellow of the inaugural class of the Lauder Institute, from the Wharton Business School at the University of Pennsylvania. Her career followed the path laid out by her education where she honed her ability to gather data, assess a situation, and design a system to optimize the outcome. This background prepared her to apply these skills to a new discovery.

Similarly, Martin used his education in Computation from the University of Manchester, the premiere British education in computer science and research in the late 1970's, to parlay into a career in software design, development, and systems implementations. His education taught him the importance of the rigors of research and application of the scientific process. His career as an early employee at Oracle, Sybase, and Yahoo taught him the necessary skills to take new, transformative ideas out to the world successfully.

By virtue of their education and work experience, Susan and Martin were uniquely poised to take this discovery, deepen the research, and from there produce an actionable system. They worked hand-to-hand with over 7000 research subjects. Each person was interviewed and documented, and from these interactions Susan and Martin distilled the most true and accurate descriptions of the Natural Numbers. Through their teaching and training they developed a transformational process and a tested system. They have now tested and implemented their system in their own courses.

Through workshops offered to organizations like Montana State University Department of Public Health and Human Services, Montana Conservation Corps, the Dappersmith Group – a New York Based branding consulting firm – and the Department of Corrections for Lewis and Clark County, they have continued to develop the applicability of their system.

Susan and Martin were invited to teach at Esalen, a transformational retreat center in Big Sur, California, where they are now on staff as regular presenters. They have taught and spoken internationally, having offered events in Oslo and London.

One of the goals of this book is to illustrate, through the work conducted thus far, that we have sufficient evidence to suggest that our hypotheses and process are viable: there are nine physiologically different kinds of people, identifiable through a simple physical process, administered by a trained professional, that takes into account a variety of physical attributes and abilities.

The essential goal of this book is to provide tools and information that will enable an individual to self-identify their Natural Number by reading and studying the Natural Numbers in this book. Body of 9 will be offering a confirmation process that includes support and training once you have self-identified. Our on-going research will look at the effectiveness of the self-identification process compared with the facilitated process used to date.

Theory of the Natural Numbers

There is a formal process that is followed by any reputable scientist in order to bring awareness of new knowledge into the world. Known as scientific inquiry, this process gathers observational data, forms a hypothesis from that data, and then tests that hypothesis by comparing its predictions to the results. Susan and Martin have used this process to gather data and develop their theories. Their predictions reliably match the outcomes, making their hypothesis become a theory. The evidence we have gathered in the testing of our hypotheses has thus led us to the Theory of the Natural Numbers.

It is important that a hypothesis or theory propose an idea that can be falsifiable; otherwise, it isn't very useful. Simply proposing that everyone has a Natural Number isn't falsifiable, as that statement does not define what a Natural Number is, how many exist, or how to test for their presence.

The intent is not to avoid scrutiny by posing such untestable hypotheses. For instance, the initial observation that there are nine Natural Numbers can be falsified through experimentation: if a person has a Natural Number never discovered before, or doesn't have any detectable primary Natural Number of the nine, the premise would be invalidated.

There are three such component hypotheses that underlie the theory of The Body of 9, and guide the research process.

Hypothesis 1

Each person has nine physiological centers in their body, one of which is born active. This active center we call their primary Natural Number, and it shapes their physical and sensorial reality. It is the 'nature' in the 'nature versus nurture' aspect of our development.

Findings to Date:

Hypothesis 1 evolved from our work offering Natural Number identification broadly and without cost, inviting anyone who was curious to have the identification experience. Since 2012, we have worked directly with more than 8000 people of dozens of nationalities, races, and cultures. Using our physical identification process, to date we have not found anyone that does not have one of the regions active as their primary Natural Number. This has been concluded from:

- The participant's physical and energetic experience of the identification.

- The participant's ability to resist physical pressure when in the various postures, or produce and mimic specific movements without training.

- The development of musculature and tissues in the participant as correlated with moving from a specific region of their body.

- The participant's alignment with the described attributes of the identified Natural Number.

Natural Number crosses race, culture, and nationality. In some regards, you have more in common with any person who shares your Natural Number than with any member of your family. It does not matter where you are from, how you were raised, or your genetic origins – to date, everyone we have encountered has a Natural Number, and exhibits the distinct traits and characteristics necessary to identify, activate, and strengthen their access to that region.

The bulk of our research has been in the United States, but we also have data from 42 countries across Europe, Scandinavia, Great Britain, South America, Russia, Asia, and Australia. Natural Number is a human, body-based reality.

California and Montana are where we have done the most Identifications. In California we did most of our Identifying at festivals where people gathered in large numbers and were open to trying the Identification experience. In Montana, where we have lived the last five years, we have made a concerted effort to get a high percentage of the Bozeman population Identified.

Our research indicates that Natural Number is relatively evenly distributed in the population. Certain numbers appear to show up more frequently in different occupations, or at different types of events, but as of yet we do not have conclusive data for these observations. California distributions are fairly similar to Montana distributions. Looking at the pie chart below you can see the distributions by Natural Number are fairly even, but the Natural Numbers 1-4 are slightly higher making up almost 50 percent of the Identified Population. At this point we do not know if that is representative of the general population or of our sample size. As we broaden our research answers to these questions will be revealed.

Natural Numbers By Percentage

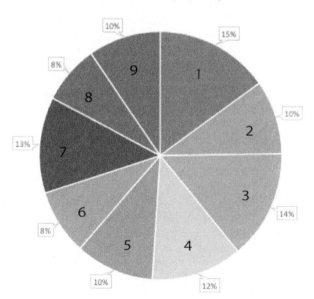

Hypothesis 2

Within a set of two people who are romantic partners and the children that they produce, none will have the same Natural Number, until there are eight or more children born to the same biological pair.

This observation is more difficult to prove on a larger scale, as it requires accurate identification and documentation of the children and their parents. This concept, however, is not necessarily unheard of. There is some evidence in historical documentation that reflect references to this theory; for example, Westcott[4] wrote in 1890: "Very curious speculations as to the relation between Numbers and marriage, and the character of offspring from it, are to be found scattered throughout the writings of the Philosophers."

Until now, there hasn't been an ability to quantify or measure these family to Natural Number relationships. Since 2012, Susan and Martin Fisher have been gathering evidence in identifying and tracking family groups, with the intent to present these observations in the years to come.

Findings to Date:

1. We have not identified any procreating couples who share the same Natural Number.

2. We have not seen a duplication in Natural Number between biological parents and their children until it becomes mathematically necessary (i.e. there are already nine nuclear family members, with all nine Natural Numbers represented).

3. This aspect becomes more complicated when miscarriages and early childhood deaths occur between siblings. Because we are not sure at what point before birth the Natural Number is defined, we do not know whether a miscarriage at some period of

---

[4] *Numbers: Their Occult Power and Mystic Virtues,* W. Wynn Westcott. First Edition 1890: ISBN: 1-56459-316-9 p. 20.

gestation would influence the birth order of Natural Numbers in a nuclear family unit.

4. In families with adopted children, as well as blended families, we have seen duplication of Natural Numbers between parents and children and siblings, indicating that this phenomenon is biological.

5. In observations to date, twins, and all other groups of children gestated together, do not share the same Natural Number. We postulate that this is one of the reasons people can tell identical twins apart.

We are continuing to study these patterns, gathering more data about birth sequence in families.

Hypothesis 3

A person's Natural Number does not change over one's lifetime. It can first be observed in newborn babies and becomes more evident as they age, expressing fully in the early teen years.

Findings to Date:

Due to the bulk of this research having been conducted within the last decade, this is currently difficult to confirm, but has been observationally true thus far. As we gain more data points tracking the progress of children through adolescence and into adulthood, conclusions will become more readily available. In addition, whenever we identify a person, we use photographic evidence to support our identification. Photographs from youth are particularly valuable in this verification process.

Whenever we encounter someone again, post–identification, we confirm the accuracy of their original identification. There are times when we recognize a mistake with our original assessment, as the process is still evolving. We believe these are errors in the identification process, rather than changes in the person's Natural Number; in some cases, the person in question will testify that the original identification had not resonated as strongly as the second. As our accuracy in identification improves, so will the ability to test this hypothesis.

Assertions

We also have some assertions that may become part of the hypotheses and ultimately theory:

Assertion 1

In order to be able to identify and support the Natural Number of another person, you must be able to create that activation in your own body at will. For those who are learning to identify people's Natural Numbers, the initial evidence suggests that achieving full activation of all of the nine Natural Numbers precedes the ability to identify accurately.

To date, we have not yet seen any person – nor any system – that can identify someone's Natural Number accurately more than 40% of the time *unless* the facilitator can activate and hold all of the Natural Numbers active in their own body. Once the facilitator can activate all regions of the body at will, their accuracy rate typically increases to about 80-85%. This accuracy rate improves with time and experience as the person masters all aspects of recognizing and strengthening the primary Natural Number of others.

Susan learned to activate all nine Natural Numbers in her body, and it was this ability that allowed her to readily observe this phenomenon in others. Once Susan had a sufficiently powerful experience with each Natural Number, she was able to create at-will activation of each region. She was then able to learn more about each Natural Number, using her body to observe, experience, and make sense of all nine.

Assertion 2

People experience greater fulfillment in life when they can activate all nine Natural Numbers.

Anecdotal and observational evidence suggest that people who have had their primary Natural Number activated feel happier and more relaxed within a year of the initial activation. People that can activate all regions of the body are calmer and more perceptive of others. The evidence suggests people begin to hear and respond to their deepest self – and make decisions from a more authentic place as a result. They are better able to distinguish between their natural gifts and talents, as opposed to their learned skills and behaviors. They come to understand their differences in approach and the strengths they offer as compared with others. This lends to a sense of purpose and self-confidence.

Research Challenges

Currently, it can be difficult to identify another person's primary Natural Number without specialized training, direct contact, and an equally skilled partner to observe the process. However, we are working on automated methods to allow anyone to be identified regardless of circumstance.

There are many factors that contribute to recognizing the different Natural Numbers. Makeup, plastic surgery, physical injury, disabilities, weight changes, alcohol and drug use, and trauma – to name a few – can obscure physical evidence. Eyeglasses also significantly obscure the quality of a person's eye contact.

People of the same Natural Number also rarely congregate in large groups. This makes it difficult out in the real world, where we operate, to see the similarities and differences between the Natural Numbers. When witnessing a group of people of like Natural Number, the similarities of the physical attributes become much easier to recognize. But they disappear in the complex variety of our social circles.

Future Double-Blind Testing: The next stage of scientific proof will be double-blind studies. The challenges this presents involve a volume of test subjects and trained identifiers; in addition, technology is not currently available that could facilitate automated Natural Number identification.

The Observational Data

The process of identification involves the observation of body shape, face shape and muscular hold, eye shape and quality, the center of movement, energetic signature, and the ability of the person being identified to hold a specific physical posture.

Since 2012, we have recorded our interactions in our database, which details everyone with whom we have worked directly – currently more than 7000 people. We have also identified another 2000 by photographic/video evidence. Natural Number has been shown to be evident in people of 42 nationalities, all races, and all ages from babies to senior citizens.

From study, conversation, and anecdote with these thousands of individuals, we have distilled the core commonalities that apply to each of the Natural Numbers – their focuses, their gifts, and their challenges – in terms that resonate powerfully for each group. Our descriptions reflect the language, energy, and core values as described by a Natural Number's own members. The words are chosen carefully, as is the manner in which the information is presented. As a result, in the cases where we have worked hand-to-hand with new participants, we have been able to describe their life experience with an accuracy that surprises them and their friends who are there to observe.

A Summation of Findings

Since 2013, we have been researching, documenting, and refining our knowledge of the skeletal/muscular differences between the Natural Numbers. Each Natural Number uses a particular combination of bones, muscles, and fascia as part of their body's movement center; the result is a distinct differentiation in how certain structures of the body develop in each Natural Number. The phenomenon can also be observed in how different people "lead" their movement from different regions of their body. For example, in the image of a person with Natural Number 3 (presented later), you see a raised and rounded clavicle where the top rib goes underneath the clavicle and connects to the manubrium. While we are not sure if the act of lifting at the manubrium creates this raised collarbone, or the raised collarbone is there to support that lifting of the manubrium, it is something that we consistently see in the body of Natural Number 3s.

When seen repeatedly among members of a group with the same Natural Number, the physiological differences become increasingly visible and pronounced. We were able to expand these points of reference at festivals in particular, where we would work with up to 100 people per day. The repetition of people with the same primary Natural Number showed us the specific patterns in each of the physiologies.

We also developed large collections of photos demonstrating people's expression of activation and consolidated them on Pinterest, a platform particularly suited to the display of images side-by-side. When examining these photographs, you can recognize patterns and consistency within the Natural Numbers.

The data gathered to date supports our theories and assertions. For instance, as mentioned earlier, observations on Hypothesis 2 show that so far, no one in a nuclear family – parents and their biological children – share the same Natural Number until there are more than nine people in a family. The eighth and nineth child share the energy of their parents, and there is some evidence that children from the tenth on start to repeat the same sequence already represented in the family order.

Also, as reported earlier, the geographic distribution by Natural Number around the world appears generally uniform, although some events, gatherings, or professions seem to attract more of certain Natural Numbers than others.

We have learned that people of each Natural Number use the same words to express vastly different concepts and physical sensations. Often, it is only through activation of a Natural Number region in the body that a person can truly begin to comprehend the physiological experience that informs another's use of language to describe their perception; if ignored, this reality holds a possibility of miscommunication.

The particular findings for each of the nine Natural Numbers are detailed in each Natural Number-specific chapter.

The World Context

Where Nine Show up in Other Systems

The study of numbers – the relationships between them and their interactions with human life – has been documented since our earliest records of civilization. Many ancients preferred to use numbers instead of words to describe complex ideas, as the same word could mean different things to different people. Each of the numbers from one upwards are associated with specific attributes.

In the modern world, numbers and equations form a basis for describing the laws of the physical world, such as gravity, thermodynamics, and topology. Certain ratios, such as pi and phi – the latter better known as the "Golden Ratio" – have a tendency to reappear throughout mathematics, art, and natural sciences. Even our computer coding languages have their root in a binary system of ones and zeroes.

No matter the era, numeric relationships have been used as often as words and images to model our reality.

The number nine occurs in symbolism throughout history and across continents. This list summarizes a few of these systems:

1. Pythagoras used his learning from his travels to found an esoteric school based on the philosophy of numbers.

2. The Enneagram, a personality model based on nine personality types, called Enneatype, was developed from knowledge brought back from Asia in the 1900s, perhaps based on learnings from the Sufi religion.

3. The Catholic faith (specifically the Jesuit Priesthood) has been aware of and has used the Enneagram for a long time.

4. Pope Gregory in AD 381 in *Homily* 34 describes nine orders of Angels.

5. There are nine Muses in Ancient Greek mythology.

6. There are nine Sabine Gods, from a pre-Roman group of people in central Italy.

7. There were nine gods of the Etruscans.

8. MacCaulay's poem *Horatius* in 596 mentions swearing by the nine Gods.

9. The 145th Psalm gives nine reasons to praise God.

10. The 9 Elements are used in India to determine matches for arranged marriages.

11. Feng Shui is based on a three-by-three magic square, with all rows across, down, and diagonal adding up to 15. This Lo Shu Square, as it's known, is also the root of Xuan Kong and the I-Ching.

12. Egyptian temples and history describe the nine Neters, or forces of nature. There is some evidence they had nine temples, each dedicated to the study of one of the nine.

13. The Norse Eddas document nine worlds connected by the world tree Yggdrasil.

14. The nine-pointed star is the common symbol for the Baha'I Faith.

15. In Christianity, a nine-pointed star symbolizes the "Fruits of the Spirit".

16. Homer's Odysseus in his *Odyssey* has nine lands through which he journeys.

17. Human Design has nine centers included in the system.

Except perhaps for the nine Egyptian Neters, none of these appearances involve a discussion of the physical components of humanity.

Comparison with Psychological Models

Nature vs. Nurture in a Body-Based System

There are a number of existing psychological models of human interaction. Common personality assessment systems include the Big 5 Personality Model, Myers-Briggs, DISC assessment, and the Enneagram. There are also many effective therapeutic and developmental systems available that can be highly effective for personal growth and development, systems like Landmark, The Hoffman Process, Mindfulness and Meditation, and many more.

We are often asked what differentiates Body of 9 from other systems, philosophies, and advisors.

The first answer is that Body of 9 is a **context** for understanding where and how the other systems and philosophies fit into the whole of our human experience. The nine Natural Numbers each have fundamentally different wisdom, skills, and value sets. This means that any system or wisdom that originates from a subset of the nine will not be complete and whole. Rather, the subset of wisdom will likely reflect the wisdom of the Natural Number(s) from which it came. It will resonate for you if you share a Natural Number, or you are particularly needing the wisdom of that particular Natural Number. We think that this is the reason that most self-help books and systems typically reach 11% of the population – or $1/9^{th}$.

The second answer to the question about what differentiates Body of 9 is that it is also **a body-based modality** with physically actionable things that you can do, that do not involve thinking. You learn through your body, and the activation of the regions of each of the Natural Numbers.

There is a critical difference between the Body of 9 process and traditional personality typing and classification models; your Natural Number is identified through a physical process, informed by your body's physiology, instinctive responses, and movement. Indeed, Body of 9 is primarily a body-based system that secondarily identifies innate strengths, gifts, and attributes common to the group of a particular Natural Number. Psychological testing methods rely on answering questions on behavior – physiology is not included.

Without delving into the age-old debate of whether nature or nurture is "more important", the distinction between body-based grouping (nature) and response-based grouping (nature and nurture) is necessary to understand for many reasons.

Determining your personality profile involves a very different process than determining your Natural Number. The personality typing process may involve observing and documenting your behaviors, or answering a series of questions. The results are heavily influenced by your life experience, or nurture influencing the original nature. These influences include family, culture, ongoing social interactions, media, education, religion, politics, and other such circumstantial factors. Such personality assessments can be informative and valuable, especially when revisited over the course of years to witness personal change and growth.

In contrast to psychological typing, Natural Number is identified through outside observation of the body's natural structure and responses. We see it as a "hardwiring", unchanging through the lifespan. A person's activated region influences their means of perceiving and engaging with the world, determining some specific innate strengths and qualities. In this sense, Natural Number can serve as a stable touchstone in the midst of life's ever-changing complexities, biases, and crises of identity.

In summation, members of the same Natural Number group are united by physiological structures – their Nature. Life experience may impact the expression of our personality, affecting our behavior, humor, passions, pet peeves, etc. This will produce a variety of results within one Natural Number group when tested using personality models – their Nurture.

The Enneagram

The system that is most directly comparable to the Body of 9 is the Enneagram. We see at least a 40% correlation between a psychologically tested Enneatype and a person's Natural Number when a person has used both identification methods.

The Enneagram came to the West via George Gurdjieff and subsequently through the teachings of Oscar Ichazo and Claudio Naranjo. The Enneagram has developed into a method of helping people understand themselves by looking at the behaviors that get in their way. Helen Palmer, is the author of *The Enneagram: Understanding Yourself and the Others in Your Life*. In her book she tells us that the group of Gurdjieff's students who brought this knowledge to the western world decided that the best way to tell a person's type was by looking at their phobias and negative personality traits.

In understanding and describing the Natural Numbers, we do not look at behaviors or experiences – we look at commonality of skills, values, physicality, and energy signature to determine a person's Natural Number.

While the initial observation of the physiological differences of the Natural Numbers was based on a version of the Enneagram Test and the martial art Aikido, the understanding of how the Natural Numbers manifest has evolved significantly through our research over the last ten years.

The Enneagram Identification Method

There are several ways of determining your Enneatype, either through a panel of experts, observation, or self-selection using questions or type descriptions. The Enneagram typing method thus depends on observational or self-answered questions on personal beliefs and behavior.

There are certain challenges posed by this process. A person's view of their self and the world around them is unavoidably shaped by their biases. Humans often select information that fits into their vision of reality, in a documented phenomenon called "confirmation bias."

From the "nurture" perspective, we are raised by people of a different Natural Number, who often expect us to be like they are. Since Natural Number does not repeat in families with less than nine people, as has been observed, it follows that our family members do not understand how our bodies are different from theirs, and how those differences affect who we are and what we care about. This means we are rarely effectively supported in our strengths. This in turn can manifest artificial doubts and phobias that could skew the results of a self-reported personality test. We may also struggle to admit to our true phobias and weaknesses when left to such self-reporting; it can be easy to pick what we would like to be or think we should be, as opposed to what we are.

Also, if one has done substantial work on oneself, through therapy, coaching, or another healing modality, the nurture and the phobias may no longer line-up with how we see ourselves.

Is My Enneatype the Same as My Natural Number?

Based on our work with hundreds of people who know both their Enneatype and their Natural Number, it is not common for a person's Enneatype to directly match their Natural Number. Identification of one's Enneatype often reflects the way a person has learned to cope through the experiences and traumas of their life. We see the Enneagram as a reflection of the nurture, rather than the nature of an individual. Enneatype is determined from behaviors, whereas Natural Number is determined by your physiology and how your body develops. While the Enneagram has great value, it is not a perfect predictor of Natural Number.

Working together to understand the relationship between your Enneatype and your Natural Number, when they differ, can be a very healing process. People have found great value in knowing their Enneatype as something different than their Natural Number. It shows where you are in relation to where you started. Understanding both, and when they differ, can be a good indicator of a pathway back to who you are at the level of your authentic self.

Myers Briggs Type Indicator

According to the MBTI website: "The purpose of the Myers-Briggs Type Indicator® (MBTI®) personality inventory is to make the theory of psychological types described by C. G. Jung understandable and useful in people's lives. The essence of the theory is that much seemingly random variation in the behavior is actually quite orderly and consistent, being due to basic differences in the ways that individuals prefer to use their perception and judgment.

Perception involves all the ways of becoming aware of things, people, happenings, or ideas. Judgment involves all the ways of coming to conclusions about what has been perceived. If people differ systematically in what they perceive and in how they reach conclusions, then it is only reasonable for them to differ correspondingly in their interests, reactions, values, motivations, and skills."[5]

Interestingly, if you remove introversion/extroversion from the system, MBTI becomes a model based on nine variations in personality. Extroversion/Introversion (E/I) is not a determining factor in Natural Number. A person can be anywhere on the E/I spectrum for any Natural Number. Introversion and extroversion seem to be part of the nurture rather than the nature of our development, or are at the very least an independent factor. We do not see these as indicators or attributes of your Natural Number.

No research between the correlation of MBTI and Natural Number has been conducted at the time of this book being written, so we do not know if the MBTI minus E/I is a good indicator of physiological nature. If the other categories of indicators come from the natural way of being, there could be a correlation. At this point, it has not yet been determined.

---

[5] The Meyer Briggs Official website: https://www.myersbriggs.org/my-mbti-personality-type/

But, as with the Enneagram, MBTI is a model based on personality and behavior – nurture, not nature.

Body of 9 Provides a Physically Actionable Path

The main challenge with personality and nurture-based methodologies like MBTI or Enneagram versus Natural Number is that they don't provide an actionable physiological path to understanding yourself and others.

The route to using these psychological models is through intellectual understanding – thinking. Empathizing with the perceptions or values of someone with a different MBTI or Enneatype requires practicing patterns of thought radically different to one's own. There is nothing to be lost in enhancing one's ability to communicate honestly and non-judgmentally with others; however, the use of the Body of 9 offers a more physically actionable approach to the process.

Humans are physical creatures. We improve our bodies through physical action. For example, reading a book or even watching a video on how to play tennis won't teach you how to return a tennis ball across the net. You'll have a general sense, but will require in-person training to reliably play the game. Learning to activate all nine regions in your body is a similarly physical practice, one that enables you to perceive, and to some extent share, the physical reality of others. It reaches towards that same goal of connecting with people of different minds, but through a body-based series of exercises that we can physically feel and comprehend.

Body of 9 and Trauma

Understanding your Natural Number and the Numbers of those in your family of origin can provide valuable insight into the dynamics of how trauma played out in your life. It can shed light on the moments you were supported or not supported at the level of your most authentic self.

Knowing your Natural Number alone will not heal the injuries. If you suffer from past trauma, it is incredibly important that you seek professional help and learn healthy coping mechanisms to handle the manifestations of that trauma.

We define baseline readiness as a general state of presence, an awareness of self and balanced emotional condition. This is a place where trauma is not leading us through our lives. Once at baseline, developing a new relationship with your body by learning about your Natural Number and how to activate the other eight can be extraordinarily beneficial. It readies you to live a life of purpose, abundance, and compassion. It marks the beginning of a new journey toward exploration, expansion, and transformation.

There is evidence that different kinds of trauma affect people of each of the Natural Numbers in different ways. For example, when even-numbered Natural Numbers dissociate, they lose connection to the source of their body-based wisdom. Trauma affects them somewhat differently than it does the odd-numbered Natural Numbers, whose source of wisdom comes from their access to more non-physical wisdom. Understanding the Natural Number system is extraordinarily valuable in a therapeutic setting.

Ready to find out about your Natural Number?

We have presented the benefits, the research and the context for understanding your Natural Number. Now it is time to dig into the specific physiologies, attributes, skills, and gifts of the nine Natural Numbers.

Read through each of the following Natural Number sections. Try the exercises, consider how it would feel to be supported as described in each section. Do you look like the people in the pictures? Can you move as described? What resonates for you?

One you have a good sense of which of the Natural Numbers is most likely your own, then it is time to get your self-identification confirmed. For information on the next steps on your journey visit our website: Bodyof9.com/bookinfo

Users' Guide to the 9 Natural Numbers

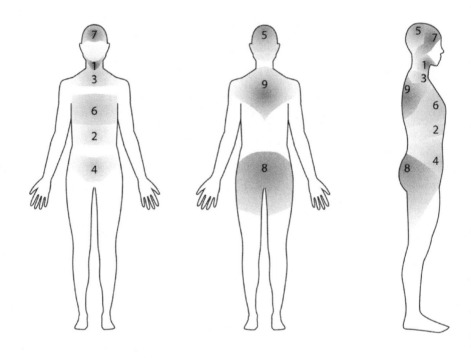

How to Use this Section

In the following chapters, each Natural Number is described in depth. Each Natural Number specific chapter includes:

1. The specifics of the body structure, posture of activation, facial structure, use of the eyes, gestures, and other physical markers, all detailed as clearly as possible

2. A description of the skills, values, and abilities of each Natural Number.

3. Suggestions on how to be in a relationship and work together with each Natural Number.

4. Suggestions on parenting, which will teach you about how to support children with each Natural Number.

5. An exercise to help you learn to isolate and activate the part of the body for that Natural Number.

6. A checklist of the key physical and non-physical attributes for you to use to self-identify your Natural Number.

Remember that each person within each Natural Number group is unique in their life experiences and behaviors that come from their nurture. This means that some markers and attributes may have different expressions between individuals, and may not apply to every person; however, there will be a preponderance of evidence that builds a case for understanding how your body informs you and where you fit into the larger picture of humanity.

The information in these chapters comes from the people we have worked with over the years. In group discussion and personal interviews, we have distilled the consistent messages and physical characteristics from their responses to an array of questions and topics. The descriptions and the specific words have been tested many times with people of each of the Natural Numbers to be sure that they resonate as powerfully as possible.

As we mentioned earlier, the challenge with language means that, while you may find that you share the characteristics described in these chapters with many of the Natural Numbers, understanding the specific intent and context of the words comes from having a true physical experience of that Natural Number. In a sense, there are nine definitions for many commonly used words, such as energy, intuition, spirit, Source, connection, engagement, and consciousness. These words each mean something very different depending on which Natural Number is using them. As you read, ask yourself if the way the word is used – and what it is attempting to describe – makes any sense to you.

We would first like to offer our definition of "Source" so that readers may insert their vocabulary of choice as they read. Source can be substituted for God, the Universe, Energy of Creation, Cosmic Energy, Life Force, or whatever term you use for the definition-defying, all-encompassing energy, bigger than any one of us, affecting creation and all things that are. In the case that none of these terms are appropriate for you, we suggest you consider using the word Nature.

We would also like to define what spiritual means in the context of the Body of 9. Spiritual is not religious in our context. It refers to the nonphysical – that which we perceive with our Natural Number region that is related to our greater purpose, to the "More". The odd numbers typically have a more specific focus on the nonphysical than do the even numbers; keep this in mind as you are reading the descriptions.

We specifically want to address the parenting sections; in many cases, there may be apparent overlap, implying that the suggestions that are good for one are also good for another. This is, of course, true; good parenting in the broadest sense includes understanding how unique your child is, holding boundaries, and keeping them safe. But there is a difference, perhaps subtle but important, in how these aspects are used, what is supported, and why you employ them that makes the purpose of the action different. Read the parenting section while thinking about your child of that Natural Number to better understand how they are different than you and different than your other children, because it is very unlikely that your children share a Natural Number with you or their siblings.

If you know your Natural Number, start with your chapter to build a deeper understanding of the amazing attributes and abilities that come with your physiology. Practice activating your Natural Number region through the exercises at the end of the chapter. Begin to learn to trust, honour, and invite your Natural Number to guide you in your actions, beliefs, and ideas.

If you do not know your Natural Number, we recommend that you read all nine chapters on the Natural Numbers, then review the last page of each chapter and select the Natural Number that you most identify with. From there, go to our website bodyof9.com to look for opportunities to have your Natural Number verified and activated. Identification is the first step on the journey toward understanding and living from your innate being.

You can experiment with the information and exercises in the chapter to see if they make sense and are relatively intuitive for you to perform. Do you experience a shift in your consciousness when you try the exercise at the end of each chapter? Is it easy and calming for your body? Do you feel validated and seen on a deeper level than you've experienced in the past? Do you see the physical characteristics of that Natural Number in your own body? If the answer is yes to all of these questions, and you would like confirmation, contact Body of 9 to set up an Identification Experience.

The information here is not designed with the intent of being read cover-to-cover. You are of course free to do so, but take your time digesting and making sense of each Natural Number. If you know the Natural Number of someone with whom you are familiar, think about them as you read the chapter about their region. This will help you understand both the Natural Number and that person at a deeper level.

As the people with even Natural Numbers live more inside their bodies, and the odd numbered are less bounded by physical reality, you might find some of the descriptions in this section difficult to accept. Since there really are nine different kinds of people, this is to be expected, but throughout our journey of discovering the nine Natural Numbers, the mantra of "don't disbelieve" has served us well. Eight out of nine people have no experience of your reality, so it makes sense that they probably have a reality that, up until now, has not been adequately understood by others. Stay open, as you read through these sections.

We hope that you will find this information useful in gaining a deeper understanding of the Natural Numbers, and of their function. The Natural Numbers are designed to work in community as a whole. Each performs a specific function that must be held in the context of the other eight, receive input from the other eight, and assist the others in their respective functions. When we learn to play our part in harmony and connection with all nine Natural Numbers, our gift becomes clearer, receivable, and invaluable in the whole.

Natural Number 1 (NN1)

To know the beauty of the source of creation is to know the perfection in the imperfections. From here, we know that all of creation – and all beings within it – are equal, and should be treated with respect and honour.

Physiology

Body Structure

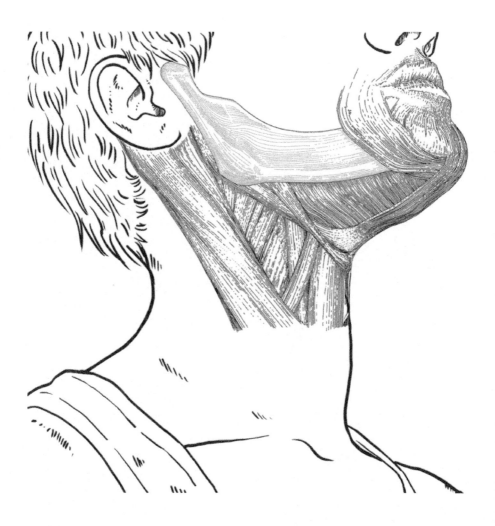

Natural Number 1s use a stretch of the spine at the back of the neck combined with the gentle rise and forward extension of the chin, creating a light tension in the throat under the chin as they make receptive eye contact to connect with others. When the throat is opened in this manner, the jawline moves up, parallel with the ground. The muscles of the throat, under the chin, become taut, supporting and balancing the body.

Posture of Activation

To activate NN1, stretch up at the back of the neck and make a slight movement of the chin up and forward, opening the throat. The muscles under the chin and at the top of the neck fire gently; they tighten without straining, creating the activation of the throat. Once the throat is active, NN1s connect to Source and bring energy into the world through the throat and eyes. The eyes soften to strengthen and activate the connection to that Source energy. If the person with NN1 is making eye contact with another person, the receptive and vulnerable gaze creates a heartfelt connection, creating a profound sense of wellbeing and beauty, honouring the other person.

Facial Structure and Expression of Activation

In the facial structure of NN1s, the jawline is typically very distinct: a straight line down from the ear, usually longer than in other Natural Numbers, with a defined turn into a straight jawline, out to the chin. The jawline will be parallel to the ground when the chin is lifted into the position of activation. This distinct jawline and lift make the neck look elongated when compared with others.

The mouth is relaxed, set in a gentle upside-down arc, though not in a frown. The lips are gently drawn down from the pull of the activated throat. A smile is not part of the facial expression of activation. The muscles of the cheeks and forehead are neutral and have no contraction or particular expression.

Eye Quality

When the chin is raised, the eyelids naturally come down to a half-open position. This creates receptivity in the eyes. As the connection builds through the activation and eye contact with another, the eyes take on a receptive sparkle.

When NN1s do not wish to make a connection (consciously or unconsciously), they may keep their eyes wide-open, preventing soft receptivity. If this is combined with the chin lift, it can look defensive and uninviting to others.

Muscular Tone

Most people who embody NN1 have lean bodies, of which they are not particularly aware. Body tone is developed only if they have chosen to exercise regularly or develop a particular physical practice. They are typically very gentle; the vulnerability of opening the throat makes the body willow-like, relaxed, and non-defensive when NN1 is active.

The rest of the body structure varies depending on life choices and experiences. Often, NN1s stay lean over the course of their lives. There are exceptions, especially in the case of underlying traumas, struggles with mental health, or other situational factors.

Gestures and Movement

The movement for NN1s starts and balances at the throat. When they move, the throat will engage first, leading and centering the movement. NN1s will often lean forward to open the throat if they are not comfortable with opening it through the chin lift.

Hand and arm gestures are typically high, at the level of the throat, with the hands working in a fluid, rolling motion, coming out from their throat center. They use the whole hand, punctuated with a gentle forward pulse from the throat while engaging the chin. The gestures are not typically sharp or directed (unless the person is angry or upset).

With the throat leading the movement for NN1s, you may see a pulsing movement from the throat, or a rolling of the head and shoulders around the throat when they speak, sing, or dance. As mentioned earlier, they may lean forward to create the opening of the throat.

Activation and Its Sensations

When a person with NN1 has their Natural Number activated, and they make extended connection through the gaze with another person, the connection is very vulnerable, honouring, and open. As people of NN1 allow you to see them, they invite you into a timeless, limitless connection, which can begin to feel like you are floating together.

For both people in an NN1 eye-to-eye connection, a profound sense of ease in being together develops as the connection deepens, sometimes giving a sense that you both have had many more connections than you initially realized. A person's face may appear to "morph" in front of you when you stand with someone in this manner; participants have described shifting colors, proportions, and a flowing of features as boundaries become blurred. As the connection grows, the eyes may water, both from non-blinking and from the power of the connection. It is important to practice not blinking, as each blink resets or weakens the connection.

When people are in connection with NN1, they become more aware of the energy of creation that flows through people into the world. Activating NN1 allows you to feel the importance, and purity of others. As you become aware of this energy, everything becomes profoundly beautiful, and feelings of awe and wonder fill your being for wherever or whoever receives your attention.

As the initial connection is building, it can be very uncomfortable as people meet their natural resistance to vulnerability in the presence of another. Once the connection is established, however, it becomes more comfortable, honouring, and timeless; you may feel as though you never want to break the connection.

Focus

When NN1 is active in the body, there is a sense of blurring the lines between reality and Source. There is a deep feeling that you have value, that you fit into the overall human purpose, and that everything will ultimately be okay.

The soft focus in the eyes is enhanced by the energy of the connection through the throat. Visually, everything else drops away in a hazy, ethereal manner while connecting with another person.

NN1s have reported that when they are creating (writing, singing, speaking, painting – whatever their chosen medium is), there is a sense of slipping into that ethereal, timeless space. NN1s also desire to draw out and help others feel the same sense of beauty and value in the creative expression.

In the Real World: Reflections on Being a Natural Number 1, by Branson Faustini

"The best feeling I can think of is getting to know someone and seeing them for who they truly are. NN1s eagerly open up the deepest, most insecure parts of themselves (sometimes probably a bit too quickly) in the hopes that other people will open themselves up (which rarely happens to the extent hoped for). I think NN1s often confuse this with a desire to be understood.

I think that a lot of NN1s have a feeling or voice inside their head that tells them "no one will ever understand you on that level". It's a very negative voice, but on some level it may be correct. I think some NN1s look for validation by looking for someone to understand exactly what happened to them.

But what they really want inside is to have someone open up completely. The other person's issues could be completely different – they don't even need to speak the same language. All that matters is the integrity, the openness, and the honesty of that connection. It could be as simple as someone crying in front of a person with NN1, or just silently watching the sunset together.

A blade of grass is a blade of grass, a junk pile is a junk pile, a homeless person is just another person. NN1s experience awe and beauty in the context of the blade of grass; I have to clarify that this context is not some deeper meaning that everyone is cut off from – it's there for all to experience, and it is something that NN1s help others to know.

Things aren't beautiful because they are perfect or imperfect – that's a misnomer. To NN1s, things are beautiful because they are exactly what they are.

The spiritual connection to Source brings the context that lets us see things without the baggage of our own lives. I guess NN1s can put themselves in anyone or anything's shoes if they open themselves up enough to Source. Just like any other Natural Number, NN1s can look at a sunset and say: "Oh, it's just another sunset." Connection to Source is almost a choice, in a sense. It's not a eureka moment; it's a decision to let pure empathy into your heart.

The perfection is in the precision of nature and life.

I think this fascination comes from the miracle of that intricacy – how complex, interlocking systems align together: bacteria live in the dew, the dew is drunk by an insect, the insect is eaten by a bird, the bird is eaten by an owl, etc. – but I think that specific kind of fascination is different from connection to Source.

Some NN1s become fascinated by those ideas. Without an open connection to Source, they can become extremely analytical. They experience wonder in the knowing of how something works. I experienced this a lot earlier in life, where I would try to explain myself and my experience to others – WHY something was incredible – and I'd get hung up on the science of it rather than the feeling of it.

I think that a person with NN1 who is connected to Source no longer worries about the perfection in the precision. They know nature's going to take care of that part for them.

It's different when NN1s are trying to recreate that perfection. They become frustrated in the drive to achieve that absolute perfection that they see elsewhere, but when NN1s are connected to Source, they focus less on absolute perfection and more on the things that really matter to them: namely, love, integrity, fairness, and beauty."

Values, Skills, Talents, and Challenges

Core Values for Natural Number 1s:

Appreciation: NN1s intrinsically know the value of beauty, people, life, and circumstances. They recognize the changing nature of creation and appreciate its harmony and balance.

Acceptance: NN1s love people as they are, where they are, and who they are. They know that people are doing the best they can with where they are right now. They know deep in their being that all people are equal and should be honoured.

Connection: NN1s value deep sustained connection at the level of the essence of life. They recognize and connect with the essence of our being, inviting and enabling us to understand our existence. They value being fully present to the connection with you in this infinite moment.

Creativity: NN1s are driven to express their understanding of Source, beauty, and value through their creative powers. This can be in any medium or talent they choose.

Skills and Talents

NN1s enable people to feel their connection to something larger than themselves (Source, God, a higher power, nature, energy – whatever word a person uses to describe this).

NN1s' ability to help others feel and see the beauty of the person in front of them – and the world around them – helps people to know that they are part of something bigger. It creates a starting place. Once connected to Source or spirit energy, humanity is ready to move and change from a place of honouring and equality.

NN1s experience awe and wonder in the context of the simple, the mundane, or the magnificent. They are moved by the incredible circumstances that came together to create its existence – the continuous cycle of life from death, of annihilation to creation to annihilation. The visual component of perceiving with awe and wonder is a powerful prompt, but it is the intense empathy for the duality of all things that creates the sensation of awe for NN1s.

This ability to perceive gradations and differences enables NN1s to point out the natural beauty and awe present in the world around them. Everywhere NN1s look, they see the good in juxtaposition with the bad, the beauty with the ugliness, the joy and the sadness. They live a life experience of paradox, and this starts as soon as they are born.

This discernment enables them to know that life is simultaneously beautiful and ephemeral – full of value and importance, yet fragile and flawed. Their NN1-ness tells them that all beings should be honoured, treated with respect, and offered the simple dignity and right of existence. In order to help others to experience this awareness, they have a core level of vulnerability. Through their body's expression of this vulnerability – the opening of the throat and connection with others through a receptive and honouring gaze – they share a profound feeling of the goodness and rightness of our human experience.

If we allow NN1s to see us through extended, vulnerable eye connection, they will help us know that we have the goodness within us, and that, despite the paradoxical experience of life, we get to experience the beauty of existence. This exchange can happen only with NN1s when their center is active, when they feel safe, and when they choose to allow you to see who they are and to see you in return.

Challenges

The biggest challenge for NN1s is not to compare themselves to the perfection of the Source of creation. When measured against this perfection, everyone will fall short. NN1s can fall prey to a sense of unworthiness.

It becomes important for NN1s to understand that, at some level, they have been chosen to help all of us know that it is okay not to be perfect. They help us know 1) that we are perfect as we are in this moment, 2) the process of creation itself is perfect and 3) we are the product of this perfection but do not have to match it. Having worth in who we are is the gift we offer. NN1s help others to know this, but often find it hard to believe it about themselves.

Another challenge that NN1s face, which they may or may not consider a challenge, is the constant striving to create beauty and to measure up to the beauty standards of the world. They can seek to beautify themselves, constantly reaching to match that perfection. It is a very slippery slope that can send them into a spiral of despair and a belief that they lack value if not properly understood.

In the Real World: Susan and Natural Number 1s

"At Burning Man 2018, I had the opportunity to identify more than one hundred and twenty-five NN1s, eighty-five of which were males, mostly in their thirties. The experience of standing on my identification mat in our camp tent at Burning Man with so many NN1s was utterly transformative. It takes a little longer to identify NN1s because the connection builds over time. The more time I spend with them in the connection, the more powerfully they feel seen and met. This more powerful experience allows them to take this experience of activation home in their bodies in a more sustainable way.

As a result of working with up to fifteen NN1s a day for ten days, I took the activation of NN1 so deeply into my body that I didn't default back to my Natural Number 6 immediately, and that NN1 became a place that I could occupy for long periods of time.

Toward the end of that festival, I witnessed a conversation between three beautiful men with NN1. All three were in their mid-thirties, powerful, fit, attractive. The conversation was about how to change the narrative in their heads about themselves and how they fit into the world. They began the conversation by acknowledging the narrative that is classically held, especially by male NN1s (although woman are not immune): "I am not worthy, I have no value, I am not good enough, or perfect enough; no matter what, I deserve the bad things that happen to me – in fact, they are probably planned by the universe."

Their discussion centered around how they could develop a practice around first noticing when their inner voice went into the downward spiral with the negative narrative. Instead, how could they consciously choose a new narrative that is positive and supportive of themselves? They realized that, for the good of the world, they needed to find a new way of dealing with their internal "you are not perfect" voice. From this Burning Man, Martin realized that NN1s don't hear the whole message. The message from Source is, "You're not perfect – I love you" and NN1s tend to ignore the "I love you" part.

As we exited Burning Man 2018, I began to feel the loss of the deep connections I had made in NN1, knowing the opportunity for them was fading as we drove away, back into the everyday world. For the first time I deeply understood what NN1s felt and how that negative spiral could be devastating. It sat right alongside the connection to Source – and I had a very hard time moving into my normal Natural Number 6 place of action. I felt my imperfection, my self-judgment, and my insignificance in comparison to the majesty of Source and the intense loss of connection. I had to find a new way to release myself from this comparison so I could return to functioning in the world. To do this, I needed to learn a combination of connecting all the way to Source, using my body to release the negative thinking. As I regained my connection to my Natural Number 6 way of being, these feelings subsided. But this newfound understanding helped me to empathize with and support my friends with NN1 in a more compassionate and deeply connected way. Our capacity to connect, to receive the gifts of others, can be expanded as we allow ourselves to go deeper into the activation of the other Natural Numbers. But it is new territory!"

Natural Number 1s Interacting with Other Natural Numbers

Some things for NN1s to remember when with people of other Natural Numbers:

1. Your desire to know others profoundly may not be met with the level of openness that you offer to them.

2. The connection that you make with people comes from being vulnerably available. You know it takes time to establish the profound NN1 connection. Give people time to adjust as you offer the availability of the connection. Allow yourself to be seen in the connection.

3. When you hear that negative voice inside your head, realize that it is part of the duality of your experience, and not a true representation of your value. Remember that you are loved, by Source and by people. Look for how to express those feelings to yourself in a positive way.

4. Recognize that another person's comment is not necessarily a criticism of you, even if it may feel that way in the moment. Try another perspective on the comment or ask for clarification without using defensiveness.

5. If you wish to make a connection, take down your defenses and show your vulnerability; don't hide behind a mask. Make and hold eye contact receptively with your chin raised and throat open.

6. If you do not wish to make a connection, then avoid eye contact and keep your chin down.

7. You do not always have to be open for a connection, but the task of making the connection will likely fall to you if you want to create one. (This is less true of people with Natural Numbers 2, 3, or 4, but they will appreciate that you have offered to initiate connection with them.)

8. Other Natural Numbers may not value manners, politeness, and the honouring of others as powerfully as you do. They may, as a result, do things that you may disapprove of or be disappointed with. Try not to hold others to your standards or apply judgment to their behavior. Remember that they care about very different things than you do. Be an example, not a critic.

9. Your core sense of self-worth, of having value, won't be satisfied by success in competition, but will come from your creations, especially if they aren't quite perfect. Remember, you have been chosen to show us that it's ok not to be perfect.

For Those Who Don't Have Natural Number 1

How Others Support Natural Number 1s

Remember that NN1s already have a built-in sensor of right and wrong, good and bad. This built-in moral compass is there for them to discern and express the value of something.

1. Be positive and supportive. There is generally no need to criticize or correct NN1s. Most of the time they have already done that for you. All you are likely to do is reinforce any negative thinking that they have already started. If you are in a position of mentorship, be gentle and supportive when addressing mistakes.

2. Meet NN1s with your true, vulnerable self. They want to know the real you.

3. Make sustained eye contact, allow them to see you, and hold the connection even as it becomes intense.

4. If you feel judged or criticized by a person with NN1, let it go as best you can. It is most likely that they are actually criticizing and judging themselves.

5. Keep your signals regarding approval and support consistent. If you praise one thing and criticize something else that is related, it all becomes criticism.

6. Honour and respect your NN1s, and do not make fun of their vulnerability and gentleness.

Parenting a Child with Natural Number 1

Children with NN1 see others in a deeper way; they want and need deep connection. The desire to be seen for who they really are is too deep to keep bottled up for a long time. If it's been bottled up long enough, it can explode out at the wrong time (or situation) towards people who aren't ready for it. When this aspect of their being is belittled, they can lose confidence. They may develop disguises for who they are, in an attempt to hide their vulnerability.

Children with NN1 know when they have done something that is not right or doesn't meet their standards of perfection/precision, and they will begin at a very young age to use this ability of discernment to judge themselves. Whenever you as a parent express disapproval or disappointment over something, your child will internalize it, and they will begin to allow their own inner voice to become the voice of the critic. Thus, it is very important to use support and encouragement to teach and discipline NN1s; don't reinforce the trauma by using disappointment. Their internal voice may start them down a spiral of despair about their worthiness as a human being. It is not necessarily easy to notice this happening from the outside. They present a very gentle and beautiful exterior that often masks a truly harsh and self-deprecating internal narrator.

There is an internal voice inherent to NN1s that constantly reminds them: "You are not perfect". This is the ironic side effect of their Natural Number: they see and know the perfection of our infinite being, but they only know themselves at the level of an imperfect human being. The human being that they are does not measure up to the infinite being that they believe they could be. Thus, even as they are driven to help others recognize their perfection and worth, they will struggle to see the same in themselves. Ensure your child knows their value. It is critical that the parents of NN1s reinforce that not being perfect is better than okay – that there is also perfection in imperfection, paradoxical as that may seem to us non–NN1s. It is their gift to remind us that none of us are perfect and that our Source knows and loves us for that imperfection. Remind them of the "I love you" part of the "You are not perfect; I love you" that they experience. It is unconditional love.

We have talked to many NN1s and have heard a shared sentiment that is interesting. In the back of some NN1s' heads, when something bad happens to them or they feel stressed, there's a tiny sensation that feels as if the bad thing was *meant* to happen to them. As if it was written out before they were born – almost like destiny.

Ask your children how they feel; ask them what they say to themselves about the things they have done or experienced. Help them develop a different internal narrative around themselves and their comparison with the beauty of life force energy surrounding them, focused on love and approval and appreciation for the imperfection of their humanness.

There is a particularly special quality to the beauty that comes from the gentle and honouring way of NN1s. This manifests as an open vulnerability that must be supported and nurtured. Teach your child about posture and the use of the eyes. Encourage them to open the throat, activate the muscles under the chin, and receive people with soft, receptive eyes. Make and hold connection with them; honour who they are. Be sure to explain that they only need to cultivate connection with others when it feels safe to them.

We have noticed that children with NN1 quickly pick up that having their chin raised and eyes soft is not how others behave in the world around them. They will begin to modify their posture to reflect more common postures, bringing the chin down and opening the eyes more fully. They may open their eyes wide or break eye contact as a defense mechanism to keep people away. You might see them lean forward, leading with the chin to get the activation in the throat without lifting. Encourage your NN1 to openly use the physical ability of their posture of activation, reassure them that this is not only ok, it is important.

Others can perceive the NN1's vulnerability of honest connection as weakness rather than power, bringing out the bully in peers or the abuser in adults. If NN1s are bullied and abused, they can also become bullies, sometimes the cruelest bullies of all with their discernment of imperfections, towards both themselves and others.

NN1s that suffer from abuse of any kind will not likely tell anyone about it. If you notice your child's behavior changing drastically in any way, consult an experienced therapist. We most often see children with NN1 turn in on themselves. They begin to believe that they have no value as a human being.

Keep an eye on your child's interactions. If anything happens to reinforce their internal belief system that they are not perfect and don't measure up to external standards, they can begin to suffer from a sense of worthlessness. Prepare your child with positive responses to being bullied or being treated unfairly. Help them know that the bully does not have power over what they believe about themselves, and that they have the choice of how to respond.

We tend to push our children into competition. Sometimes they push themselves into it as way to measure their self-worth. NN1s, because of their natural ability to discern, know when they are doing well and pleasing others. They do not like disappointing the important people in their lives. When this turns into winning at the expense of others, it takes them away from their connection to their deeper purpose: the honouring of all, equally. While they may do very well in competition, it does not necessarily serve the development of their sense of purpose and self-confidence.

If your child is interested in sports and competition, or any high-performance endeavor, focus on how great a teammate they are, rather than on the quality of their performance. Focus on how they honour their teammates to bring out the cohesiveness of the community.

Here is a story from a person with NN1 about his challenge with competition:

"When I was a kid, my dad was a soccer coach and I had to be on the team. I never tried in the first place because I didn't feel coordinated and I felt like I'd never be as good as any of the other kids on the team. I really enjoyed sitting on the sidelines and talking to the other substitute kids on the bench. My dad was never mad at me about this, but I do remember knowing that he was disappointed. I wished that I could play well but I didn't try in the first place because I felt that I'd just let him down more.

Something I've noticed about NN1s is that they can be stubborn, about not trying new things. They're either afraid that they'll mess it up or that they'll disappoint the person who's pressuring them, but it's something that I think all NN1s need to work on.

Fear and judgment are literally robbing them of life experiences. I think NN1s do that with mundane stuff, but they can also do it with things that would be incredibly good for them, such as a cool spiritual journey or going out with friends."

You might notice that, when your child is in competition, other kids begin to bully them, and when that happens, your child may start to shut down. If you can, it is best to address the bullying without drawing attention to your child and their experience publicly. Teach them that a bully is just trying to get them upset so they are not able to do what they need to do in the performance.

Help your child stay focused on the magic of how they are able to help people feel. They help others see the good in themselves and those around them. Keep reminding your child that this is their magic – the special gift that they offer to others – the gift of seeing and honouring others for their essence and perfection. Also reminding them that when things don't come out the way they envisioned, this doesn't mean they have failed, and it is not a reflection of their value as a person. Their value comes from within and from Source. It is not tied to the well-being or happiness of others in their life.

When is Activating Natural Number 1 Useful or Helpful?

When you first meet someone, doing so with NN1 active will enable you to profoundly honour, respect, and connect with that person. This will begin the relationship on equal and respectful footing. The relationship can go in almost any direction if the foundation starts here.

If you have lost your connection with someone, activating NN1 will help re-establish the even ground and diminish the conflict. Even with telephone calls, your activation of NN1 can create a connection and help people transition out of a defensive or combative mindset.

If you find yourself judging other people in a negative way, activating NN1 will reconnect you to the beauty and majesty of a person or circumstance, enabling you to see the good, the beauty, and the rightness of it. When the connection is not fully established, this is when judgment and negativity will creep into a relationship. Stay with the connection all the way through.

If you are interested in beginning a creative process, NN1 is a good starting point. Open your throat, connect with the majesty of Source, and then use that connection to Source to begin the flow of inspiration.

If you are mediating a situation where one party has more power than another, bring NN1 into the space to equalize the dynamic so that all parties respect the value of the others.

Exercise to Gain Awareness of NN1

NN1 is most powerfully activated when in connection with another person. You can work on the posture and your awareness of the muscles by connecting with yourself in a mirror to get a sense of what it feels like when the right musculoskeletal areas are activated.

If you wear glasses, remove them and position yourself so that you can see yourself as well as possible. The glasses will interfere with the connection. This is true for the mirror exercise and with another person.

In the mirror: Stand in front of a mirror, ideally a bit less than an arm's length away. Make and hold eye contact with yourself in the mirror. Take your index and middle fingers on each hand and place them on the back of the neck at the occipital lobes, to help you lift at the upper back of the neck, stretching the top three vertebrae, and creating space in between them. With your neck stretched, bring your chin up and forward without compressing your neck. Bring the attention to the muscles under the chin, at the top of the throat. If you move the bottom of your tongue around using the hyoglossus muscles, you can feel how to make these muscles taut. Place the tip of your tongue on the roof of your mouth in the soft-palate area, if that helps.

Your eyes should naturally be half-opened in order to keep your gaze where it was before the chin lift. Stay in this position, but do not strain, holding eye contact with yourself in this position for as long as is comfortable. Notice the use of the muscles and the quality of your eyes. You should see a shift to a receptive quality in your gaze.

With another person: Stand facing the person – about an arm's length away, but close enough that you can meet hand-to-hand, palm-against-palm, and still have your arms bent comfortably, with elbows supported by your sides. If you are holding tension in the hands or arms, let go of this tension and relax – there should be no tension in the body outside the throat area.

With your neck extended, bring your chin up and forward without compressing your neck. Bring your attention to the muscles under the chin, at the top of the throat. As in the mirror exercise, make the muscles under the chin taut. Your eyes should be soft and receptive. Check that they are half-opened to keep your gaze on your partner's eyes.

Hold this position and think about sending energy to the other person through the throat area, focusing on one of your partner's eyes. Try to blink minimally; each blink restarts the connection. If the connection becomes intense, feel free to close your eyes for a moment in order to center, then return to the connection. Be willing to allow the other person to see you. The connection can be quite profound. Stay in the connection as long as is possible and comfortable.

In the Real World: A Caveat from Susan's Mom, NN 1

"Susan's enthusiasm after she had been identified as an NN6 was truly life changing. It was as if bells rang and rockets went off for her. She kindled my interest in this identification process and what it might mean for me. So I went to CTI Leadership to find out my Natural Number. I remember it well. We were a large group and I watched eagerly as each person was identified. It was interesting and informative as the group of varied people were identified with their Natural Number.

At last, it was my turn. Various pushes and postures were tried on me, and finally I was identified as having NN8. I was immediately crestfallen and confused – so opposite of what Susan had experienced. But, the expert had spoken, and no one questioned it. I was resigned to having NN8 and accepted my fate. But I did not like or enjoy the experience or feel seen and validated as had been so true for Susan.

This was many years before Susan acquired the skills of being able to identify one's Natural Number, and years before Susan and Martin observed that people with the same Natural Number never marry or have children. So, I spent almost ten years believing I was an NN8, uncomfortable and doubtful.

Then one day I went to Susan, photograph in hand, saying to Susan, "this is one of my favorite photos of your dad and me." By this time, Susan could identify readily and with great skill. She looked at the photo, and began to go through other photos of me where I consistently raised my chin and exuded a soft joy from my eyes. Susan had been having questions regarding my identification and had been looking for an opening to talk with me about it. Susan declared, "Mom, let me work with you again!"

That is how my NN1 was Identified! Suddenly everything made sense. I felt comfortable with the words and descriptions that fit into the pockets of who I am. Up to then, I had to take someone's word for who I was – but it never resonated. Once Susan awakened my NN1, I felt the aligned truth in my body. Today I am a big supporter of Susan, Martin and their work."

Natural Number 1 Checklist:

Physical

1. Throat is open with slightly raised chin where movement is initiated.

2. Eyes are soft and receptive when activated; eye contact is valued and important to create the connection.

3. Body tone and shape is varied but relaxed.

4. Jawline comes straight down from below the ear and takes an almost 90 degree turn so that when the chin is lifted, the jawline comes parallel to the ground.

Nonphysical

1. Help others to know they have value.

2. Know that all beings should be respected and honoured.

3. Understand that we must be vulnerable to be truly open to others in connection.

4. Value the creative process and see the beauty in the simplicity and rightness of creation.

If you identify with Natural Number 1 and would like to verify that this is indeed your Natural Number, visit our website for more information and the next steps on your path: https://bodyof9.com/naturalnumber1

Natural Number 2 (NN2)

Engaging – connection for the sake of connection, without agenda – is magic. Engagement is there to support us being ourselves, in the moment, with each other, no matter what.

Natural Number 2 Physiology

Body Structure

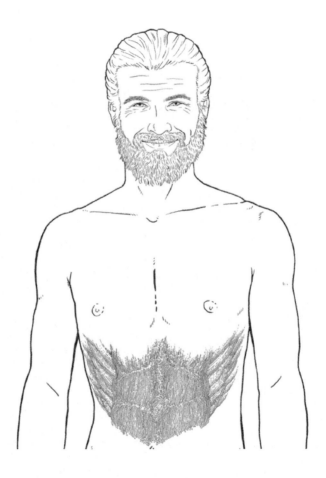

Natural Number 2s balance using the muscles of the upper abdominals. They have a tremendous flexibility in the middle of their body, just below the ribcage. Making the upper rectus abdominus muscles taut enables them to feel and adjust to what is going on in the body of others.

Posture of Activation

Natural Number 2s (NN2) move and connect with others using the upper rectus abdominus muscles. When engaged, the upper abdominals are pushed out and taut, so that they vibrate with the connection. The entire body is ready to be with whatever is in front of it and comes even more alive with movement and an engaged relationship. Eye contact is also part of the activation for NN2; through direct eye contact, they engage with others, inviting them into an easy and fun connection.

NN2s use the body to continuously adjust as the person in front of them adjusts, merging and matching with the person they with are in the moment. Through attuning their whole being to the body of another person – for the joy of connection alone – they create a profound and meaningful engagement.

People with Natural Number 2 merge with others so strongly that they liken it to an energetic entanglement. This action creates a readiness in all parts of the body to be with whatever is present. They are primed to move, to respond, to match whoever they connect with. It is this responsiveness to others that enables them to change as the person in front of them actively changes. This makes physical movement an important element of the posture of activation.

Facial Structure and Expression of Activation

The face of a Natural Number 2 is neutral, and the eyes are bright, clear, and available. Unlike many other Natural Numbers, the neutral state does not lend to a particular expression; the tone is even and relaxed. Nothing occurs in the face that could present a barrier to interacting with them. They smile easily; even when neutral, their lips curl up at the outside in an open expression, indicating they are ready to engage and smile with you.

The face has even spacing throughout all regions; the eyes are slightly wider set than average, and the ears appear lower vis-à-vis the eye when in the neutral position. There is a wider gap visible at the temple between the eyes and the ears, keeping the spacing around the outside of the eyes, nose, and mouth more uniform. Typically, the forehead is longer/higher, and more rounded at the top.

Neutral Expression:

In the neutral facial structure of Natural Number 2s (on the previous page), the muscles are relaxed, holding an open and available expression. Their expression holds no immediate hint to their internal feelings, especially anything that would indicate a lack of availability or hold another person away. The eyes are clear and alert, attentive to you, inviting but not demanding contact. If you choose to engage, they are available, but they will not force a connection. Once connected, the face will shift from neutral to engaged.

Engaged Expression:

When Natural Number 2s are engaged, their eyes sparkle, and their cheeks pucker up and in toward the nose. A full smile may or may not be part of the engaged expression of activation, but the lips curl up into more of an invitation to deepen the connection.

Eye Quality

The eyes of a Natural Number 2 are usually more almond-shaped. In their neutral state, they are opened wider, and have a clear and available quality, not communicating any preconceived ideas, agendas, or expectations. They are simply present and ready if you choose to engage. When they connect, the eyes narrow and sparkle, the outside of the eye dropping slightly.

Muscular Tone

Most people who embody Natural Number 2 have natural tone in the upper abdominal muscles. In the above photo, you see how much tone and control a person with NN2 can develop in those muscles. They can also easily isolate and slide the ribcage horizontally at the height of the upper abdomen, keeping the shoulders perfectly level with the hip line while the hips remain still.

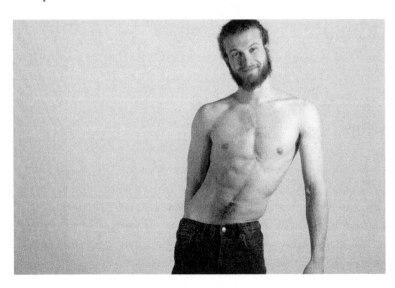

Gestures

NN2s tend to gesture around the level of the upper abdominals. They may swing their arms back and forth around this area with their elbows resting on the sides of the body, arms and hands moving freely.

Activation and Its Sensations

NN2 becomes active in connection with something or someone; they can connect with people, the environment, nature, and animals. NN2s are constantly exploring the entanglement of everything around them, wherever their interest draws them, or with whomever they engage in an active connection.

When NN2s engage in the connection, it feels as if the rest of the world drops away. There is a sense that who we are in the moment is totally okay – there is no need to change, and, if you do change, they will be right there with you. As the connection grows, it becomes easier and cleaner, reaching an effortless place, where what wants to happen in the relationship starts to happen. If you are willing to stay engaged with NN2s, they will make it as energetically easy to be with them as possible. All they ask is that you show up as who you are and stay engaged in the connection as it intensifies and develops.

Focus

When out in the world, Natural Number 2s are always available and ready to connect with others; the invitation is ongoing. NN2s merge so completely with others that they often lose their connection to themselves, and struggle to differentiate between self and other. This creates a feeling of oneness and togetherness when the connection is active: only you and they are in focus.

When the connection ends, it leaves a gap, but the threads between the person with NN2 and the object of their connection remain. Unless they are actively severed, this makes re-establishing the connection easier. We call it entanglement because it is so relationally complex that differentiation between self and other becomes challenging.

This can be exhausting for anyone, and NN2s are no exception. To recover, they require the alone time – the quiet time – that is needed to reconnect to self and make sense of what happened in the relationship with another. Knowing the difference between self, the relationship, and other becomes the art of existence for NN2. They must learn to shift their focus from the connection to themselves to differentiate from the interaction.

In the Real World: Susan's Experience with Natural Number 2

"Childhood is a very interesting time for Natural Number 2s. They come out of the womb looking for connection. They open their eyes sooner, and constantly crave and ask for eye contact with their family. When my youngest daughter, an NN2, was born, she came out with her bright eyes open and looking for me. She knew me and was searching for me as soon as she was born.

Her sisters, Natural Numbers 8 and 7, had easily played on their own, and enjoyed toys like the bouncy or rolling chair. She would have very little to do with anything that separated her from the family. As an infant, at dinner she would cry until we put her up on the dinner table where she could see us while we ate. As long as she was included, could make eye contact, and felt a part of the connection, everything went smoothly.

I don't remember her learning to walk; she spent most of her time on my hip or on the hip of her godmother. She bonded so strongly with her godmother that she considered us both to be her mother.

One of the most important aspects of parenting her was to keep her well-fed. If I missed a meal with her and she got hungry, she would get super upset and throw a tantrum. When I didn't anticipate her needs and take care of this basic need, it would push her over the edge. I am not sure this was conscious, but it was so important to her. Her sisters were not like this at all. They would tell me when they were hungry or take care of it themselves. I have heard similar stories from other mothers of NN2s.

When she went to kindergarten, she was sure no one liked her. After I spoke with her teacher, it became apparent that she was actually one of the most liked and sought-after kids in the class. Her understanding of how to treat others was already so developed that she couldn't imagine that the other kids actually liked her because they didn't interact with her the way she interacted with them – adjusting to what they needed and wanted.

In first and second grades, she was often placed in groups with other kids who had trouble behaving properly. Her teachers did this because she was able to relate to anyone and brought a connection and camaraderie to the group. She thought she was a "bad kid" because she was so often paired with kids with challenges.

Another thing I wish I had done better for her was to understand the rules of engagement for the moms of her friends. I was a loner at the time, avoiding social contact. The impact on her was significant. If a mom wasn't involved with the other class moms, then their kids were left out, too. She attempted to get me involved, but she wasn't yet sophisticated enough in her communication skills to get me to understand the social implications for her. It wasn't until much later that she was able to articulate this importance to me."

Values, Skills, Talents, and Challenges

Core Values for Natural Number 2s:

Engagement: They offer an invitation to be fully present in the connection; nothing else matters in that moment. They are looking for meaningful engagement.

Dynamic Harmony: It is important to people with NN2 to create dynamic harmony through the connection. They are able to adjust to and enliven the connection with another person, as the person changes dynamically through the interaction.

Movement: Through movement, both at the cellular and muscular level, they understand what a person needs, how to be with them, and how to engage in the relationship. They have a personal need to be moving, which creates a sense of being alive. Movement in dynamic harmony with the world is an NN2's way of interacting.

Skills and Talents

People with NN2 can choose when and how to move through the world. They meet whoever they encounter exactly where they are, and can match or mirror the person in front of them easily. They are looking to help you grow through the connection, and for this they need your fully present awareness of the relationship in the current moment. One person with NN2 describes it as, "Through connection, I give them back themselves."

NN2s have a built-in understanding of the "rules of engagement" in relationships. When active, NN2s make the people around them more aware of each other; they can impact this connection without even speaking. There is no competition in the interaction; this creates a potentially healing connection that enables people with NN2 to help others know and experience what they are not seeing in themselves. They provide the communication glue for a community, looking to maintain and repair its flow. If someone is being left out, they will often befriend that person and integrate them into their circle of friends, facilitating the missing connection for them.

NN2s anticipate other's needs, but often find it hard to state their own. They don't understand how people can completely ignore the needs of others, not realizing that other Natural Numbers, must learn through practice and experience to understand the cues that seem obvious to an NN2.

Challenges

NN2s often express that they have a hard time knowing themselves; they merge with others so completely that they lose who they are and become the connection instead. This becomes challenging when the connection ends, creating a deep sense of loss, and the feeling of being adrift without identity. They put the connection with others ahead of all else, forgetting to maintain their relationship with themselves. The most important relationship for an NN2 may be with themselves. It cannot be neglected, and although some NN2s don't like mirrors, mirror-work can be a valuable tool for connecting to and strengthening their understanding of themselves. Growing this sense of identity becomes very important for NN2s as they build a life of their own. If they do not learn to differentiate themselves as an individual from their merged relationships, they can become confused and disappointed in their friends and family.

Disappointment is a challenge for NN2s in a larger scope as well. They know how deep and beautiful a true engagement can be, and they are always striving to create that with others. The other Natural Numbers do not intuitively know how to create such a profound connection. They are often baffled and sometimes wary of the ease with which NN2s can do this. Since other Natural Numbers don't know these rules of engagement for relationship, it can be hard for NN2s to have fulfilling relationships. Others want to be with them and near them, but don't know how. It is usually very difficult for the NN2 to guide us by asking for what they need. As a result, people often back off or disengage just as the connection becomes interesting to the NN2.

When a person cannot sustain a powerful enough engagement, the NN2 can suffer frustration and sadness. They can also develop resentment from always being the one to build and sustain their relationships, which can put strain on their connection with friends and family. It is important for NN2s to make conscious decisions about which relationships they wish to invest in, and recognize that their gift in the relationship, to create a beautiful and engaged connection, is not something the other person can easily match or understand. We urge our NN2 friends to keep on connecting despite the disappointment, but to choose carefully.

In the Real World: Susan, Activating Natural Number 2

"Natural Number 2 was one of the hardest for me to learn to activate. I thought there was something I had to "do" to activate NN2. It turns out it is more a way of being than doing, and, for me as a Natural Number 6, doing was my thing. There are a lot of commonalities between NN2 and NN6, but the way they manifest can really throw you off when learning the activations. Both Natural Numbers move a lot. Both need others to be most effective. Both are responsive – NN2s to others and Natural Number 6s to energy. Both are super intense when you go deep into the activation, but the form of the intensity is quite different. NN2s' activation comes from human intensity, whereas Natural Number 6s' is energetic intensity. Both are electrifying and energizing, but in entirely different ways.

Learning that difference between energetic intensity and human intensity was really difficult for me. Human intensity is about being in the present moment with just the other person – everything else drops away. Opening to energetic intensity is at first all-inclusive, then it drills down to the specific information. It starts open, then narrows down into the specific detail, looking for the most alive energetic signature, as if Natural Number 6 is a focusable telescope into energy. NN2 starts with all of a person in focus, and then morphs into a responsive dance-like relationship, often wordless, responding to the shifts in the energy of the connection. In order to learn this, I had to tire myself out through movement to the point where my Natural Number 6 could not keep up and then give over to the intensity of NN2 connection.

No other Natural Number can be used to keep pace with another person in the way that NN2 can. No matter what happens in the connection, the activation of the body through NN2 enables other people to keep up, respond, and stay with the relationship's shifts and movement."

Natural Number 2s Interacting with Other Natural Numbers

Some things for Natural Number 2s to remember when interacting with people of other Natural Numbers:

1. Generally, other Natural Numbers have less resilience for intense human interaction – certainly less than NN2s. The other Natural Numbers do not understand how to adjust the body to keep up with the changes in the relationship, which can make staying with

these changes exhausting. This is one of the reasons that others might avoid interaction, especially when tired.

2. Natural Numbers 5 through 9 do not use their eyes to build a relationship. They use their eyes to see, to take in information for the purpose of doing or creating. This means that they may be uncomfortable with extended eye contact. They might avoid it altogether, without even realizing that they have not looked another person in the eye. When they are holding eye contact, if the relationship intensity increases, they will be more likely to look away.

3. Other Natural Numbers often use a relationship to obtain or create something. They also need structure, such as shared experiences or goals, to build a relationship. They will want to *do* something in order to establish the connection. If you meet their need to accomplish an activity while in the connection, you are more likely to be met as deeply as you would like to be.

4. Talking and moving are two ways that NN2s make relationships easier for others. Movement releases the static energy and enables another person to become synchronized in the NN2 connection. But remember that others do not know what you are doing or why.

5. It is okay to ask for eye contact, attention, and interaction when someone is not meeting you at your level. Try to avoid communicating with resentment or judgment when asking. These things are not necessarily being withheld willfully or consciously.

6. Sometimes other Natural Numbers think they are good at eye contact – but you might perceive it as staring, blank and unresponsive. This is because they do not yet know how to use their eyes to build a relationship. You can help teach them through your eye contact with them. Again, recognizing that they are not willfully withholding connection is important to the relationship.

7. Remember that your body is equipped to adjust and respond as people in front of you change, but others are not equipped in the same way. They may feel slow and unresponsive in comparison.

For Those Who Don't Have Natural Number 2

How Others Support Natural Number 2

1. Make and hold eye contact. If you make the effort in the beginning, they can make the connection easy and fun for you as it progresses. They will do all the work if you allow yourself to respond. When speaking to a person with NN2, look them in the eye – they will hear you better.

2. Allow your body to respond to the invitation to engage in the connection. Practice moving with them.

3. Pay attention; they will know if your focus wanders, even if you pretend otherwise. Be present in the moment with them.

4. Be honest when you do not have the energy to meet their intensity – the more they invest in a connection without response, the more frustrated they can feel. Ask for a rain check until a time when you will have enough energy to engage fully.

5. Show up as you, in your fullness, and they will adjust. They just want you to be you. It doesn't matter if you are happy, sad, or angry (even with them); just be there, be you.

6. Initiate connection. NN2s often feel that the responsibility of this is always placed on them.

7. Say goodbye when you leave; make a conscious ending of the connection. If you are in a conversation, don't walk away in the middle of the conversation, even if you are interrupted. To an

NN2 the connection is much more important than any action you think you have to do. Acknowledge the end of the connection with your appreciation.

8. Disappointment is the NN2 Achilles heel. If you are sensing disappointment, look to how their hopes or expectations were not met. See if you can meet those hopes or expectations more proactively. If you cannot, then explain that you can't and tell them why, so that they know that it is not about them.

Parenting a Natural Number 2

Children with NN2 are born craving connection and eye contact. From the get-go they open their eyes looking for their mother and family. As infants they want to be in the center of the action. Keep them near you and engage in eye contact. Practice sending love through your eyes to your NN2 baby.

As they grow, they may enjoy playing in an imaginative world with dolls, stuffed animals, or other toys with which they can play at relationships. As they transition to engaging with their community, you may observe that they care little for social acceptance, generally preferring to be left to carry on in their own way of being. They may also become confused by the contradictions in other people's behaviours.

They will often get along well with other children. Due to their adeptness in relationships, you may be tempted to think that your child likes everyone. However, it is important to dig a little deeper and understand the nature of the relationships to discern who they really want to spend time with. Even when they seem to like a certain peer in particular, check in with them to see if they were just being nice, or were bringing an excluded kid into the fold.

NN2 kids are very good at connecting all the other children into the community. They make friends with outsiders as easily as with the popular kids. They typically float from one friend group to another, but rarely feel like they have a "best friend." Curiously, there are also many stories from NN2s about how they befriended the kid that was left out. After bringing them into their friend group, they end up excluded themselves, often by the one that they brought in.

NN2s may think others do not like them, especially when they are younger. They feel like they are loners while others perceive them as having lots of friends. They do not like to displease parents, teachers, or friends, and work very hard to maintain relationships, rarely understanding why others are not as diligent or respectful as they are. They often interpret the other Natural Numbers' inability to build and meet them in relationship and connection as a lack of desire, when it is more likely to be a lack of skill.

Disappointment is a challenging emotion for NN2s. They would like to be met with the same level of intensity in relationships that they offer to others. When others are unable to meet that engagement level, it can be disappointing. When this disappointment is projected onto their relationships, their friends – who may be aware that they have inadvertently disappointed their friend without understanding why – may feel daunted and alarmed. Despite their best efforts, non-NN2s may not know how to fix the situation, which can then make the NN2s even more disappointed. In addition, NN2s can grow weary of always being the person who initiates the connection, and never being met with the full level of engagement that they know is possible.

94

It is very important to help your child understand how much more aware they are of how to create connections, engage in relationships, and adjust to people as they change. Helping them learn to deal with and process their feelings of disappointment will help them avoid becoming jaded and withdrawing from people.

Young NN2s understand the rules of engagement vis-à-vis school hierarchy; however, they move constantly and love to talk with others. This can sometimes get them in trouble if their teacher is very strict. If they are concerned about displeasing their teachers, they may control themselves rigidly. As such, it is important that you talk with their teachers about creating a safe environment for your child to be able to move and engage freely.

Also, your child understands that the relationships that you as their parent build with other parents is vitally important to their world. If you do not make friends with the mother or father of the person with whom they want to be friends, they know it will be harder for them to maintain a friendship with that child. If you are not part of the right parent group, they realize that they are at risk of not being included. Ask them who they would like to play with most and build a relationship with the parent or guardian of those children. It will make your child's friendships feel more secure.

Remember that your child just wants you to engage with them. If they ask you to sit with them while they do their homework, it is not necessarily a request for help with the content; it is a request for you to keep your energy focused on them. The engagement helps them focus. For non-NN2s, this is counterintuitive.

NN2s often have trouble going to sleep at night. At younger ages, they may worry that while they are sleeping you might disappear, and not be there when they wake up. When they sleep, they have to disconnect energetically; they also feel you disconnect your energy when you fall asleep. Assuring them that you will be there in the morning is important. They may also do better if they have someone to sleep with, so a physical connection is maintained through slumber and into awakening.

NN2 children can get very upset when they feel their basic needs aren't being anticipated and met. They are able to do this for others intuitively, and expect that you can do this for them; It can be very distressing when you do not. This tends to be an unconscious behavior until they reach their teen years, and from the age of two to about ten, it may instead manifest as a despairing, screaming, out-of-control tantrum that can be very scary to them, you, and others witnessing it. If you let your NN2 child get hungry, for example, they will rarely tell you that they are getting hungry, expecting you to know. This can result in them becoming far too hungry, then extraordinarily upset, so much so that they won't let you feed them. Encourage them to communicate, and continue to watch actively for their basic needs for sleep, food, or connection.

When is Activating Natural Number 2 Useful or Helpful?

For people of different Natural Numbers who learn how to create the activation of NN2, there are certain times and applications where it is very useful:

1. When you are finding it difficult to hear or relate to someone, activate the muscles of the upper abdominals and make direct eye contact, and the relationship will quickly shift.

2. If connection is missing in a community, activate NN2; use it to create more alive relationships with each person, then allow it to build the connection in the space as a whole.

3. If you find yourself feeling impatient, or judging a person as they are speaking, activating NN2 can help you listen without judgment or agenda, releasing any thoughts that might be distracting you from understanding.

4. If you want to improve connection in a relationship, practice making and holding eye contact with your NN2 active. It will help you to know how to connect, using your eyes.

Exercise to Gain Awareness of Natural Number 2

Stand facing another person, or yourself in a mirror. Start with your arms at your sides. Make the upper abdominal muscles taught, expanding them out, allowing them to support and balance your body. Keep your attention on flexing your upper-abs. Use your upper abdomen to stabilize your movement as you raise your arms. Bring your hands up, palms facing forward, until your arms are relaxed supported against your body at the elbow.

If you have a partner, join hands, palm to palm. Look your partner in the eye. Allow the relationship to grow. If you have enough space, you can add movement. Move with them, matching their direction naturally and easily, and allowing your upper-abs to connect and lead. Do not force the dance; rather, allow the connection to create the movement easily and effortlessly. If you are uncomfortable, check that you are holding eye contact, and expand the upper-ab muscles again. Relax your face. Allow your expression to adjust, match and mirror the other person.

If you are looking in the mirror, look straight at yourself, and raise your arms, keeping them parallel to the mid-body, using the upper-ab muscles to lead the movement. If you can place your hands on a surface directly in front of you and still make eye contact with yourself, allow your body to pulse into the surface. Be aware of the connection with yourself through your upper-abs.

Natural Number 2 Checklist:

Physical

1. Round and even tone in the face, with even spacing around the face outside the eyes, nose, and mouth.

2. Both the neutral and the engaged expressions are present with activation.

3. Neutral eyes that sparkle when they are engaged.

4. The ability to shimmy and slide the body at the height of the upper rectus abdominus muscles.

5. Cheeks pucker up and in when engaged.

Nonphysical

6. Engage for the sake of connection, without agenda.

7. Connect through the eyes and the upper rectus abdominus muscles.

8. Recognize that everything is about connection, and the relationship between.

9. Care that you are giving others what they need and being who you are in the moment.

If you identify with Natural Number 2 and would like to verify that this is indeed your Natural Number, visit our website for more information and the next steps on your path: https://bodyof9.com/naturalnumber2

Natural Number 3 (NN3)

What is more joyful than the connection of our souls as one? When the soul is powered through connection to the pure joy that unites us, we are ready to move forward on our true path toward our most important and powerful purpose.

Natural Number 3 Physiology

Body Structure

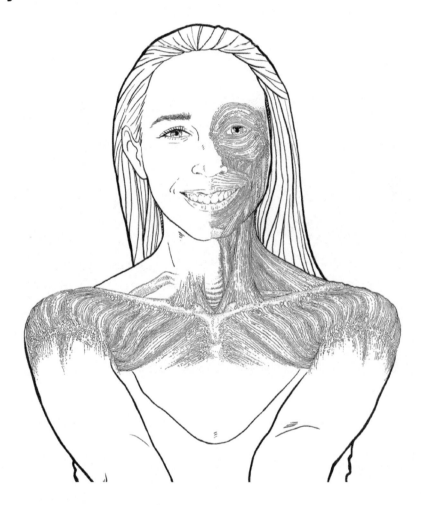

Natural Number 3's movement is centered at the manubrium – a small bone at the top of the sternum. It radiates out across the collarbone and includes the top rib, using the sternocleidomastoid (SCM) and the pectoral muscles to balance. They are the only Natural Number with a smile included in their activation. The musculature of the face activates to create a smile that moves into the eyes.

Posture of Activation

The posture of activation for Natural Number 3 (NN3) is designed to help the body create the tremendous focus necessary to unite us in a joyous connection with others.

NN3s focus eye to eye on the person with whom they connect. To create the posture of activation, lift up at the manubrium, using the sternocleidomastoid (SCM) and the pectoral muscles. The SCM and pectoralis major are the main muscles attaching to the manubrium, while the upper trapezius muscles act as stabilizers. Bring the arms up, locked out straight forward from shoulders, and set the hands palm to palm, pushing one against the other to support the lift of the SCM.

Using their amazing eye-focus, NN3s look past the layers of personality, connecting directly with the soul. When they feel the connection to and from their own being, they are able to shine the joy of this experience out to others. This brings an energetic smile to their faces that extends up through the cheekbones and into the eyes, which begin to sparkle joyfully.

Facial Structure and Expression of Activation

NN3s have both a neutral resting face, and an activated expression that includes a smile with sparkling energy.

Neutral: In the neutral facial structure of NN3s, the muscles in the face are relaxed, the cheeks are flat, and the eyes are round and focused. Often, the face shape is long and narrow, coming down to a pointed chin with very little energy in the jawline. The face draws our attention to the eyes.

Activated: When NN3s are activated in connection to their being and to another being, the outer cheeks come up. The cheeks crinkle at the outside edge of the eyes and the eyes start to sparkle as the smile engages fully, often exposing the gum above the upper teeth. The lines coming down from the nose spread wider than average and round slightly at the top. The cheeks flatten down above the nose line, but raise at the outside of the cheeks, just below and outside the eyes. As NN3s age, they often develop a secondary smile line that mirrors the bottom half of the nose lines.

Eye Quality

The eyes of NN3s, when neutral, are round, focused, and have a magnetic quality. When activated, the eyes crinkle and sparkle.

Muscular Tone

NN3s have high tone in the upper body, especially around the trapezius and pectoral muscles which lift and activate the central triangle between the arms and the clavicle. On NN3s, the clavicle noticeably rounds out and up, creating a pronounced raise in the bone, and a dip behind the clavicle. This is just above and to the side of where the collarbone connects at the manubrium at the top of the sternum.

Gestures and Movement

NN3s gesture at shoulder height or higher, often with straight arms. They may point or move their hand out from the manubrium to the vertex where their hands would come together if they were using their arms to activate the Natural Number.

In movement, they continually lift from the manubrium. Their arms move out and up, supporting the raising and opening of the chest. When dancing, they often move their arms at or above shoulder height, and demonstrate a particular upper body rotation using the clavicle around the manubrium.

Activation and Its Sensations

Connection through the eyes: People with NN3 value focused connection through direct and steady eye contact. Without sustained eye contact, they cannot create the physiological connection that channels the joy-filled energy that enlightens our awareness of our magical purpose and cosmic power.

Connection through the body: If NN3s can't achieve the eye contact needed to create a connection, they can forge it through gentle, respectful touch instead. When a person with NN3 contacts another's body, there is an energy flow of information through the touch that NN3s use to "know" the other person, or the purpose of that person's soul. This can activate the other person as eye contact would. Using both at the same time is the strongest way to be activated by a person with NN3. However, if they can use neither eye-contact nor touch to connect, they may have difficulty reading the situation, and may become confused or develop social anxiety.

When NN3 is active in connection, the eye-to-eye attention is so intensely focused that the participants' concentration on another can make the rest of the world disappear as the two seem to become one. In any extended eye-to-eye connection the outside world becomes less present. This is particularly powerful when making eye contact with any of the first four Natural Numbers, though the physical sensations created by the

Natural Number 1, 2, 3, or 4 activations are each quite different. For NN3, when the connection is ready, a state-shift occurs that brings forth a powerful energy of pure, focused, and intense joy.

The receiver of this focused source of joy will feel energized, inviting out their best self. It is as though the soul is directly contacted and empowered to know its purpose, to be ready to accelerate in that true direction. This sparks a new energy in the receiver, manifesting the intention and purpose that the person carries within themselves. This can only happen when both the person with NN3 and the receiver experience the joy and inspiration of each other.

Intention: NN3s know that there is a soul in each person and there is a soul of the universe. They are driven to enliven, energize, encourage, and inspire the souls with which they connect. When NN3s shape an intention that benefits more than themselves, they accelerate the intention into the cosmic field, providing clarity of the universal request. This is a skill that NN3s can develop through learning to be still, not moving in action or creation as is their tendency, and fully saturating themselves in the joy of life. From here, they can receive new information through the body. Their soul guides the focus of their energy, holding them steady on their path to create a better world for themselves and others.

When NN3s start to focus on this new information, it will manifest through the sharing with others. NN3s like to share the energy, to invite people into its field. They know how to articulate the details of their vision with intentional communication that accelerates the manifestation.

Focus

When NN3 is active in the body, it is electrifying. In the focused connection, there is so much joyful power that you feel as if you can do anything. NN3s are outwardly focused on the giving of such joy to others, generously and without agenda. They offer a powerful invitation to your being as their energy shines out into the world.

Their focus is so precise that they can use it to see the smallest detail, and can assemble the information of these minute parts into a much larger picture; they start small to go big. In keeping with this, they will ask a great many detailed questions to help others know their greater purpose and direction. NN3s see the sparkling possibilities ahead of us and deeply care that we too see this magic. The questions are usually designed to help others see that wondrous future, and inject energy to accelerate them toward that vision.

In the Real World – How Natural Number 3s See Detail

By Katherine Cameron, Natural Number 3

"It's kind of cool, leaving at the same time every day.

I get in the elevator. It stops on the second floor. A mom and two elementary school kids get on. When the doors open on the first floor, the mom turns to her girls (who stand right in front of me) and says "Okay, girls! Ready? Let's get this day started!" And then she holds the door and the younger child goes out. Then the older child. Then me. And she makes direct eye contact with all of us. Then she runs to the next door and holds it open for us again. Then we walk the block to our cars together.

While we do that, we pass a girlfriend and her boyfriend and their dog. The boyfriend takes the dog out early, so the girlfriend meets them at the parking-lot and he walks her to her car. They peck each other on the lips. He says: "I love you!" And she says: "I love you, too!" and hops in her car while simultaneously turning it on. Every day, right when she closes the door, he says: "Drive safe!" And I'm wondering if she ever hears it. So, he does a little "goodbye" wave and she does a smile and drives off.

I get in my car and turn on Pandora. Then I turn on the heat and start driving away. I drive past the mom just finishing double-checking her kids' booster seats and she always does two tough tugs on the seat belt as if to say: "You better be working today."

Every day. Almost the exact same. The only differences are the dog, where the boyfriend is in the yard when the girlfriend comes out, and what the older child is holding. Today it was a bag of pretzels. Yesterday it was a small craft."

This Story is a beautiful example of how Natural Number 3s use their focus and attention to detail to see and understand their world and to share the special quality of their vision with others.

Values, Skills, Talents, and Challenges

Core Values for Natural Number 3:

Generosity: NN3s use the energy of generosity to power the connection with others. By generously giving from the deepest part of themselves, they are able to activate us without agenda.

Drive: NN3s have an internal compulsion to share the energy of essence and creation with others. This creates a driving excitement, magic, and intensity that moves everything forward.

Connection through Focus: Using focus to create the big picture from small details is a great strength of NN3s. They are able to gather the deeper meaning in the energy of the tiniest particulars, and build a more inspiring, understanding vision for what is possible. They can then direct that energy toward the possibility that they see for others.

Skills and Talents

People with NN3 have a tremendous ability to focus, engaging their whole body in the experience. Through this focus, they create a connection with a person's true self and activate their magic. When they are in deep connection with another person, there is excitement and joy found in their beauty. They help us feel with our whole being, including the cosmic part of us, feeling, finding, and experiencing the magic in our life.

Through the profound and powerful connection that happens in deep-soul-level eye contact, they see into what is possible, and help us to shift ourselves into a more energized state. They can see into our future – the possibilities it holds – and help us know if we are working toward our potential. If not, they help us refocus so that we can move more directly. This ability to help us feel the magic of our cosmic selves also gives us permission to center our attention on what matters to us at that deep level.

This lends to their innate ability to turn a vision or idea into a reality. Combined with the ability to see the brightest future possibilities, they ask intentional questions to elucidate the vision, bringing others naturally to a place where they can see and share it. They stay open to possibility and are generally willing to consider new information. This channels energy into the experience and direction from others, building momentum and power. When NN3s keep the focus on the vision and inspire people toward that vision, anything is achievable.

NN3s know how to articulate the details of the vision into the intentional field to accelerate its manifestation. This also translates into the ability to give clear, visual instructions.

Once they choose to be your friend or partner, NN3s are loyal, and will keep their focus on you to ensure you are connected with your joy as a source of energy. They will continually check-in with you to re-energize or redirect.

Challenges

Sometimes NN3s' focus and detailed questioning can be seen as stubbornness or willfulness. When a person with NN3 refuses to shift their focus and continues to ask questions, this can irritate other Natural Numbers. This can also occur when they hold onto the original focus despite receiving input from others.

The smile and intensity of NN3 can also be misunderstood, or judged as inappropriate. Many more NN3s than people with other Natural Numbers have heard the expression: "Wipe that smile off your face." Losing confidence in the power and value of their smile is devastating for NN3s.

When a person with NN3 focuses on you, it feels fantastic. To be the chosen center of the NN3's world is unparalleled, joyful, and inspiring; it can also be intense and exhausting. At the same time, losing the focus of your person with NN3 can be devastating – the joy and light seem to vanish.

When a person with NN3 chooses to focus on a project, or make people into projects, it can be hard for those around them. If the person with NN3 resorts to pushing someone in the direction they envision for them, it can feel very forceful. It remains important for NN3s to stay connected with the joy and use inspiration to motivate, releasing attachment to the outcome of their role.

In the Real World: Susan and Natural Number 3s

"When I began this journey in 2001, I was in the midst of a most unpleasant divorce, and a single mom to three daughters. I spent the next seven years doing the work to heal. Finding out my Natural Number 6 was a very big part of this. Doing the work to learn about the other eight Natural Numbers and beginning to rely on what they offered was also part of this journey. I knew that I had to become whole, as me, before I entered into a rest-of-my-life relationship. In 2006, I was starting to feel ready to take steps toward finding that relationship.

I sat down with Anita, a friend with NN3, who began asking me questions about what that person would be like. She asked about every aspect of that person, each question delving deeper into clarity for the universe. Is it a man or a woman? A man. How old is he? My age. Are there deal breakers? He must be non-smoking, and not addicted to anything destructive. He must love my kids as much as me. He must have an international world-view, and be open to growth and change. He should be searching, for himself, and be accepting – if not supportive – of my commitment to Body of 9. Which Natural Number? Natural Number 5. What do you want him to partner with you on? Parenting, Body of 9, growth, and transformation. What does he do for work? It doesn't matter. What does matter is that he doesn't travel, and he makes enough money to enable us to continue to invest in Body of 9 and get my kids launched. Where do you want to live? In Marin County, probably Novato, close to where my teachers and community are centered. When do you want him to show up? Five months from now; I have a bit more work to do before I can focus fully on him.

Five months later, in early 2007, another good friend with NN3, Sue, was diagnosed with a life-threatening medical condition. She had to undergo a serious operation. I joined her team to support her through this tough time. She reconnected with a mutual friend of ours, Martin Fisher, and he too joined her support team.

Martin and I had met at work in the early 1990s, two weeks after I had married the father of my children. At the time, we were immediately attracted and became good friends. We regularly talked at work, played bridge with some work friends, and went out to lunch. At that point, neither of us was in a place to be more than friends, but it was clear that we had a powerful connection. After the birth of my second daughter in 1995 we lost touch completely. Neither of us had any idea where the other had gone, and, over the next 12 years, neither of us knew what was happening with the other. Both of us needed to go on a journey where we were challenged to the deepest part of our core — but that is another story.

Twelve years later, when I heard from Sue that she had been in touch with Martin, my interest was piqued. I was not surprised that he had resurfaced. We all had lunch together at the start of Sue's journey, and I was quite curious as to how it would feel to reconnect with Martin. At this lunch there was a thrum of interest, but again we were not quite ready, so nothing happened.

During this time, I felt that my true soulmate was lurking about. I was dating and enjoying life, feeling no pressure for change. We all supported Sue through her journey and by the fall, she was fully recovered. Martin invited Sue to dinner to celebrate. Sue invited me to join them, which both Martin and I found surprising, but exciting.

My sweet middle daughter, a Natural Number 7, came into my room as I was getting dressed for the dinner and completely changed my outfit so I looked chic, cute, and a bit sexy. I felt great and was looking forward to the evening. Sue picked me up and shone her sparkle into my being. During dinner, in classic NN3 fashion, Sue kept inviting Martin and me to shine, and that shine enabled us to see each other and ignite the spark that had been dormant. Together we all had a great time, and the soul-level connection between Martin and me was reawakened.

From that night forward, Martin and I have had this powerful, soul-level connection that would not have happened without the focus, vision, and inspiration from these two powerful and generous NN3 women. Anita enabled me to envision, invite, and manifest Martin Fisher, who met all of the criteria for my rest-of-life partner – and more. Sue helped us to awaken that soul-level connection, and generously shared her joy and inspiration with us, making our union accelerate. I truly believe this wouldn't have been possible without their initiation, inspiration, acceleration, generosity, and joy."

Natural Number 3s Interacting with Other Natural Numbers

Some things for NN3s to remember when with people of other Natural Numbers:

1. It is okay to ask for eye contact if you don't get it right away. This is not the default for Natural Numbers 5 through 9, and thus more than half the world; most people will look at you to take in information, but not necessarily present themselves as available for connection. If you don't get the eye contact, explain that you do better with eye contact – and smile at them!

2. Not everyone is available and ready for the intensity of connection that you offer. This doesn't mean that there is anything wrong with offering your full contribution. Don't take it personally when a person can't give back their full focus. If a person does not respond to your inspiring energy, remember it is not about you! They may not be in the right state to connect.

3. Inspire generously. There is nothing about your connection that is too much – in fact, it is needed. Others do not know how to manifest the same joy.

4. Generally, others will "fall back asleep" fairly quickly after you have ignited them with your energy and joy. Unless they truly embrace the direction presented by your NN3, they will need re-energizing again the next time they connect. This can sometimes become frustrating for NN3s.

5. Other Natural Numbers may feel unresponsive or resistant to your vision. Allow people to follow their process; use your smile and joy to encourage and inspire.

6. Ask questions. Your questions will lead people to see the vision and possibility that you hold for them. Allow them to create their own manifestation, with your guidance and energy. You don't need to give them the answer or push them in any direction; just light the path and energize the person from their best place.

7. Look after yourself. Some NN3s find an adrenaline rush combined with their focus to be irresistible, but eventually the rush "writes checks the body can't cash." (Yes, Tom Cruise has NN3.)

For Those Who Don't Have Natural Number 3

How Others Support Natural Number 3

Remember that Natural Number 3 is about inspired possibility, growth, and moving toward our greatest purpose.

1. If you are feeling down, find a person with NN3, look them in the eye, smile at them, and let them fill you up. The smile is a generous gift; receive and return it. Hold eye contact with focus and open yourself to the joyous energy they offer. They will make your day.

2. If you have an idea but are struggling to clarify your vision, or are simply not sure of what is possible for you, find a person with NN3 and request that they ask you lots of questions. Sometimes NN3s have anxiety, especially when joining large groups. Invite your NN3 friends to go places. Include them, bring them into the group, introduce them to others, and they will have an easier time integrating and creating the connections they crave.

3. Be willing to go deep, both in connection and in conversation. Be willing to dig into possibility and new directions. If you find yourself becoming frustrated with their focus on a singular topic, show patience, and be gentle in attempts to change the conversation.

4. Meet their eye contact. Match their intensity and let them build the tremendous power of the connection. Stay with the intensity of the experience, and do not retreat; you are safe.

5. NN3s thrive with a reliable routine that provides space for their creativity.

Parenting a Natural Number 3

Children with NN3 are born with a smile on their face, and continue to express joy easily. Their eyes are very focused, even as infants.

The most important thing that a parent can do with an NN3 child is to maintain at least ten seconds of focused eye contact from time to time; this is required for them to feel seen. If your child is upset or angry, before you begin to talk about it, hold that direct, focused eye contact. Your NN3 child can also connect to you through touch. Lay your hand gently on their shoulder and allow them to feel you. This gives physical feedback in addition to the visual.

NN3 children are very focused. It is important to allow your child to finish their activity. They hate to be disturbed when they are intent on completing or studying something. It can be helpful to create a structured and disciplined schedule, such that the NN3 knows when they must eat, sleep, do chores, or be somewhere; they are then able to choose their focus in between the structured periods. Rest and food in particular should consistent on such a schedule such that they will not be neglected by distraction. In addition, encourage your NN3 child to eat slowly; it is good for them to have practices that are paced, and manage the rapid momentum that can easily exhaust them.

It is also very important that you tell your child that they have a special non-physical gift. If they have imaginary friends, see spirits, or sense unembodied energies, this is part of their natural abilities. Other Natural Numbers do not have access to the same perceptions, and may find this strange. Encourage your NN3 not to be afraid, and to communicate consciously with a spirit if they choose, or to ask the spirit to leave if they do not want it to be there.

To help an NN3 child develop their understanding, have them focus on something in nature – a bird, a flower, a tree – for five to ten minutes. They will glimpse the spiritual energy between themselves and that object. This will teach them to open to their ability to perceive spiritual energy; some NN3s describe it as a white light, in between themselves and their center of focus. Understanding that this is their gift, to receive and share the spiritual energy, lifts the confusion that can otherwise cloud their vision. As that capacity to be with spirit expands, NN3s can learn to embrace their purpose and special abilities. This is rejuvenating to everyone involved.

Perhaps due to their ability to see the array of future possibilities when given the details, NN3 kids can worry about going to new places and environments. Morten Nygård tells a story about how – as a kid – he was invited to a sleepover that he was really excited about, but by 9pm he was ready to go home and sleep at his own house. The experience was too unknown and unfamiliar for him; he needed to get back to the familiar to feel safe. It wasn't until he reached adulthood that he could sleep out of his regular environment. On a related note, it is also hard for NN3s to get enough rest. They become so excited about what they are focused on that shifting gears into relaxation is difficult. They can become exhausted by their high energy and enthusiasm.

NN3s do better with fewer people, and can be overwhelmed by the guests coming into their home. Minimize the forced exposure to people. They may have only one or two best friends, so enable them to spend focused time with those few individuals.

116

NN3s know others and themselves through the connection; anxiety about that connection with others is a common state for NN3s. When they are unsure of what a new connection will bring, the anxiety is palpable. If the stress becomes too much, they will look for ways to escape, physically or emotionally. Because much of their internal and external awareness – as well as their sense of joy – stems from connection, these situations can leave them feeling trapped between a rock and a hard place, or if unchecked, in a vicious cycle. The anxiety keeps them from making the connection they need to know themselves, which then amplifies the anxiety. The heightened presence of the unknown keeps them from knowing, and they can run themselves ragged through physical activity while trying to reconnect with themselves at the soul level.

In these instances, encourage your child to lift up, from the manubrium. NN3s can sometimes collapse the shoulders around the manubrium, disengaging their center. Helping your NN3 child build a relationship with their own soul through focus and connection can help resist the anxieties of the unfamiliar. The ability to know themselves and address their internal experiences regardless of the situation is paramount.

NN3s may also become obsessive with being the best at something. If your child becomes obsessed with their personal performance, it is important to help them shift their focus onto something else.

Allow your NN3 child opportunities to be completely happy, and to express that happiness enthusiastically. This may feel manic compared to your own ability to feel joy and excitement – go there with them regardless, and share their full joy.

In the Real World: Katharine Cameron, Natural Number 3, Responds to Parenting Tips:

"This is amazing and awesome. I feel like my mom and I found most of this out the hard way. And some of it we didn't find out until much, much, much later in life.

I'm so happy that some parents out there will be able to see this and hopefully take it extremely seriously. It is also important for young adults. I've had to tell roommates this about myself just so our communication could go as well as possible. I'm realizing that these things need to be monitored, addressed, and handled appropriately by myself at this age.

Giving NN3s words to describe how to communicate with themselves is so important. As an adult, I can't say what I often feel inside, ie, "I will FREAK out if you schedule an impromptu meeting. I will get so mad and probably cry." Rather, I need to say, "I need things scheduled in advance as much as possible," which is so much more appropriate and understanding.

Parents and kids having this information would solve so much strife and save on so much counseling. I'm dead serious. Most of my childhood tantrums and times when I needed discipline came from a misunderstanding of these things. Most were solved by giving me a map during road trips and marking our location. Or giving me a little itinerary during vacations where my schedule would be different. And a lot of "in 20 minutes this will happen, so get to a good stopping point." So simple. But so hard to figure out on your own.

If I were to add anything it would be that new places worry me. If someone connects with me and invites me or goes with me, the fear is gone. Rooms or buildings I'm not directly invited to with connection, I get very nervous.

In prior conversations with other NN3s I know, we talked about this, and we all agreed. We'd love to be given tours of houses when we first arrive, into all the rooms we're allowed to be in.

It is not uncommon for us to get stuck in our car before going into an event, unable to move or to brave the upcoming unknown, and often too nervous to get out and try the door handle. At one event I remember, this happened to an NN3 participant. I think Martin went out and was like "Oh, hi! Come on in. Here's a seat for you!" And she was immediately relieved. All of the NN3s resonated with that feeling.

My mom tells stories about me, remembering during potty training to about second grade that I needed a tour into bathrooms, otherwise I'd opt for going outside like an animal, or pee my pants. It just created too much anxiety to enter that room without knowing what was there.

I also think we can be extremely active, and a healthy physical activity would be an awesome way in which to enroll your NN3 child. I know I could get a little crazy, and sometimes my mom would let me have a crazy dance party by myself for two hours just so I could lie down. I spent a lot of nights jumping rope in my bedroom instead of sleeping.

Our family went through a couple years of physical activity arguments. We NN3s are not lazy – we love to move. Let us choose how we want to move, and we'll become obsessed. I did not like soccer, but I loved jazz dance. Soccer didn't hold my focus and, at the end, I was so frustrated and angry that it was no good. Find my passion and I'll be an overachiever, best grades in the class, obsessed, winning competitions – but don't find my passion and I'll struggle to avoid failing.

Sun is also important to me. Nature is eye candy. I can't feel the trees being alive or anything, but nature walks that focus on using eyes to find flowers or bugs or textures are amazing and calming and mind-blowing. While there's a time and place for speed-running hiking trails, my biggest enjoyment comes from the never-ending details in the world around me. And the sun and wind combo. It's very healing. Let us look around and take some time.

Reading this literally made me cry. I feel so seen. This is probably the most profoundly "me" synopsis ever. And I really hope parents of NN3s take this seriously. Especially the little details. The looking at you. The staring at a flower for ten minutes. The slow – rather than abrupt – refocusing. This was amazing. Thank you."

When is Activating Natural Number 3 Useful or Helpful?

For people of other Natural Numbers who learn how to create the activation of NN3, there are certain times and applications where it is very useful.

1. When you want to build a more focused relationship with someone, make eye contact and hold your focus on them, allowing your NN3 to activate, lifting at the sternum and allowing your full smile to take over your face.

2. You can build your capacity for handling intensity if you practice NN3. Staying in a relationship as it intensifies is not easy for most other Natural Numbers. Practicing NN3 will improve your ability to handle intensity.

3. When it is time to brainstorm about vision and possibility, you can bring the creative energy of NN3 into the process. Practice asking questions to elucidate all aspects of what is trying to be created. No detail is too small in this process – how are those details presented so that they make the future possibility clear?

4. If you want to energize a person, group, or process – involve NN3. The activation of NN3 will bring energy into the creative process

Exercise to Gain Awareness of Natural Number 3

Alone: Stand in front of a mirror. Lift your arms to shoulder height in front of your body, placing your palms facing together in front of you with arms locked out straight. Push your palms together and lift the upper sternum and clavicle. Looking straight ahead in the mirror, look into your own eyes and focus. Bring your face forward, locking on your own gaze. Lift at the sternum and smile as brightly as you can.

With a partner: Stand facing one another, two arm's lengths away. You will each raise one arm to shoulder height and meet opposite-palm-to-opposite palm with your partner with straight arms. Lock out your elbow so the arm is perfectly straight, looking left-eye to left-eye, and focusing intently on each other. Keep your shoulders square as you face each other. Apply pressure with your palm against your partner's palm and use the pressure to isolate and lift the upper sternum and clavicle. Focus and smile. Allow the joy to build naturally through the connection.

In the Real World: Morten, Natural Number 3 and Susan, Natural Number 6

"Morten Nygård and I both had our Natural Numbers activated while participating in the Coaches Training Leadership Program. For both of us, it was a life-purpose-level call to be part of the community bringing this information out into the world. Morten and I both joined the community of people exploring this work, studying with New Equations for the initial years and have since brought all of our creative life force energy into researching, teaching, and speaking about this important information. We both left the New Equations community to pursue the research on our own, I with Martin in 2012 in the form of Body of 9, and Morten, in 2010, in Oslo, Norway, which he called Ennead.

In the fall of 2015, just after Martin and I moved to Bozeman, Montana, with the goal of being able to put more of our energy into Body of 9, Morten received an energetic message to get back in touch with me. Despite the fact that we had not talked in four years, the deep connection established between us in the prior community was still vibrant.

The energetic connection between NN3 and Natural Number 6 has always been part of the connection between Morten and me. Morten brings the inspiration and focus, and I bring the energy and direction. Together we keep each other moving, on track, in the most profound and alive direction possible.

Morten, in Oslo, and I, in Montana, talk by video link almost weekly. We check in and talk about what we are doing to synchronize our learning and direction, and to power up the energy on the core projects. The core commitment never changes for us: learn more, teach more, share more. Together we find the most alive direction and then focus the energy to manifest.

In writing this book, Morten's support energized me through my stuck periods and helped me focus more clearly on what was important. Morten's NN3 energizes my soul every week, and I help Morten focus on what is most important. We are constantly re-synchronizing, adjusting to the new energy each week, and working together to determine how the energy has shifted and what it means for us moving forward. This constant support that we give each other enables us both to stay on track, energized, focused, and having the best impact possible.

Often, together, we will make powerful energetic shifts. If I am going to put a program in place, Morten will help me articulate the value and importance of the program for others. Morten's ability to ask me the right questions elicits the most alive information, and the path becomes clear as I synthesize what has happened and clarify the next steps. It is a symbiotic cooperation — the heartbeat circulating the life force energy out into the system to manifest life and creation in the other parts of the system. Without the beating heart, the body stops functioning and all the other parts die — that is a powerful metaphor for the impact that NN3 working together with Natural Number 6 have on the system of the Body of 9.

In the process of creation, there are times when the energy is not ready to move. At these times, I will get stuck, and feel unproductive and lethargic. I really hate it! When this happens, Morten is able to re-energize and re-focus me. He will shine his joyful NN3 focus on me in our video links and inspire my soul. I may not yet necessarily know what the next steps in the big picture will be, but I will feel much better and be able to do something in the short-term until the energy starts to move again. Morten's powerful, generous, unconditional support of me and my ability to do my job as a Natural Number 6 empowers me to be my best, over and over again."

Natural Number 3 Checklist:

Physical

1. Round, focused eyes that sparkle and narrow when they engage.

2. The smile goes all the way into the eyes with engagement at the outside and top of the cheeks.

3. Cheeks flatten down when they smile; lines angle out from the nose in a fairly straight line in the neutral face. Often they develop a secondary smile line outside the line of the cheeks.

4. Lift at the upper sternum, with protruding collarbone on either side of the manubrium, the small flat bone at the top of the sternum.

5. Narrow and lean in the body.

6. Movement rotates around the manubrium

Nonphysical

1. Create and share joy with others.

2. Focus intently on whatever they care most about.

3. Inspire others to action from the purest part of themselves.

4. See the beauty in the details; asking lots of detailed questions to build the big picture.

If you identify with Natural Number 3 and would like to verify that this is indeed your Natural Number, visit our website for more information and the next steps on your path: https://bodyof9.com/naturalnumber3

Natural Number 4 (NN4)

Being our authentic selves starts with knowing who we are at the deepest possible level – this is found deep inside our being. Once that true self is known, authenticity comes from calling forth that deepest self into alignment, to be ready for connection. Trusting the wisdom contained in our bodies, from our emotions, we bring our being into authentic alignment.

Natural Number 4 Physiology

Body Structure

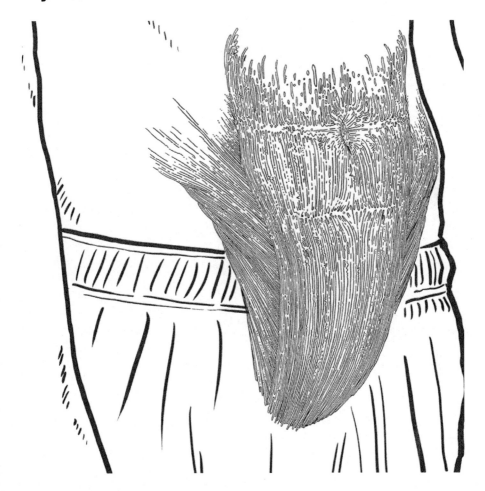

The activation center for Natural Number 4 (NN4) is located in the lower abdominals, known as the transverse abdominus. These muscles are used to balance and move the body of NN4.

Posture of Activation

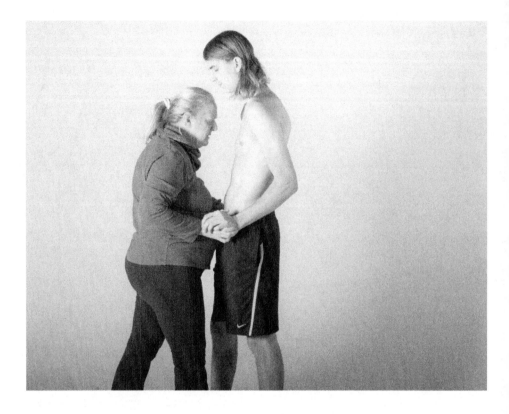

People with NN4 focus deep inside, relaxing into the muscles of the lower abdominals, bringing the lower abdomen slightly forward. Closing their eyes, they relax the muscles at the back of the neck. The breath is part of the activation; with each inhale, they breathe in the world; with each exhale, they drop even deeper inside. Once connected to their internal, timeless selves, they can expand their energetic bubble outward to include others. The breath can also be used to send the energy of acceptance to another person through the lower abdomen. In the deep space, as time slows, a sense of ease and connection descends on a person or a community included in the connection.

Facial Structure and Expression of Activation

In the facial structure of NN4s, the muscles around the mouth and jaw are soft and relaxed – there is no tone held in these muscles. The mouth is relatively straight, with the lip corners typically set just slightly below the centerline of the mouth. This does not give the appearance of a frown, but of relaxed calm.

They often hold the lower abdomen tilted forward, with the muscles of the bottom third of the rectus abdominus holding tone naturally and easily. When moving, they lead from this center, creating easy lower body movement.

Eye Quality

The eyes of NN4s have a deep, inviting quality, and may appear watery, though not tearful. NN4s blink more frequently than other Natural Numbers; when they blink, they are not simply passing fluid across their eyes, but are taking a moment to drop inside. The deeper they go, the longer they hold their eyes closed, the more time it takes them to resurface into the present moment outside of their being.

They describe this experience of being deep inside as feeling profoundly present with themselves and anyone included in the connection. The NN4s' sense of presence is about resonance with our cosmic being – our whole, deep, and most powerful self – in both the instant of connection and the continuum of our existence.

Muscular Tone

Most people who embody NN4 have fairly relaxed muscular tone in their bodies. There is an internal passion that can drive tone into the body when performing physically, but in general, the muscles in the body are relaxed, allowing the head to drop forward. When looked at from the side, with the head down and abdomen forward similar to the posture of activation, NN4s take on a sort of c-shape.

Gestures and Movement

NN4s tend to keep their hands lower than the other Natural Numbers. Typically, their gestures have a soft and gentle quality, with a fluttering aspect to their finger movement. When sitting, their shape will mimic the C seen in the standing posture of activation, and they will often place their hands on the lower abdomen. Sometimes they will place a cushion or pillow on their lap when sitting comfortably.

In dance, you will see the lower abdomen lead their movement, with the arms and hands following and extending the movement of the lower body. There is often a rolling, side-to-side hip rotation that is either separate from the rest of the body, or starting, balancing or supporting the movement of the body.

Activation and Its Sensations

Activating NN4 takes time; it is a process of bringing one's attention to the inside of one's body and mind, using the breath to drop deep into the lower abdomen.

As you drop into yourself, activating the muscles of the lower abdomen to support the descent, you may experience an initial discomfort as you hit the layers of emotion between where you typically exist and where your deepest being lives.

Through the breath and the continual descent, deeper and deeper, you can allow your body to process through the emotional layers. You descend into a space below the emotions, below the vagaries of daily life, where there is a sense of calm, peace, and contentment.

If this is done in connection with another, you can experience a sense of ease in the relationship, a realization that you don't ever need to leave the connection, and, with that, a recognition of how you are accepted for who you are. With this can come a feeling of deep gratitude. It is one of the few places where we truly experience that we are not alone – rather, here we know, in our bodies, that we are all connected at this life-force level.

Focus

When NN4 is active in the body, it feels as if time slows, and the space grows quiet; then energy deepens, pulling all present into a connection where acceptance and a passion for life resides. This is a very timeless place where only the connection matters. All of the focus shifts inside to the eternal and infinite space within.

NN4s focus on the current connection, staying in this place, in this relationship, until it runs its course. Once the connection has completed, they will gracefully end the engagement and move on to the next. This can be confusing to others; they wonder how the connection was created so deeply, so quickly, and then they wonder where it went, and why it left.

In the Real World: Susan, On Going Inside

"People with NN4 have a capacity to go so deep inside that other people wonder where they went. When NN4s go inside and do not actively include someone else in the connection, others can become very confused.

When I was a girl, my sister – NN4 – and I were hanging out. At the time, neither of us had any idea about Natural Numbers, or our differences. We were having a conversation, chatting, enjoying being together. My sister, as we were talking, closed her eyes and started to go inside. At first, I got a little angry and tried to get her attention focused back on me. She decided not to respond to me, and to play a little game to see how far in she could go without responding to me. She continued to sit there, going deeper and deeper, quieter and quieter.

I have Natural Number 6; I am super aware of the present energy, and I felt my sister suck all of her energy right out of the space, out of our connection. I got more annoyed and tried to bug her back into talking with me.

She just dropped even deeper and slowed her pace even more. The more agitated I got, the calmer and further away she went. She felt completely connected with me and was simultaneously aware of her impact on me as she went deeper into herself. But to me, she was disappearing.

Eventually, I became seriously worried that something terrible had happened to her and I called out to my mother. "Mom!! There is something wrong with my sister!" I cried out. At this point, my sister took pity on me and burst out laughing. She thought this was the funniest thing in the world.

Because we didn't know consciously about each other's Natural Numbers and how our bodies were different, I wasn't able to understand and detect what she was doing. She found her way to her place inside – her safe place – and, in this case, she realized I did not have any idea what she was

132

doing, how she was doing it, or why. She loved playing a trick on her crazy, over-energetically responsive sister.

It wasn't until I found out about our Natural Numbers some 30 years after this experience that it started to make sense. It had actually been quite traumatic for me, and, while it was fun for her, I was very confused and impacted by the experience. If I had known at the time what she was doing, the tables would have been turned!"

Values, Skills, Talents, and Challenges

Core Values for NN4s

Alignment: NN4s value, generate, and use alignment. By settling into the lower abdomen, they drop into the deep and intimate space of self, which creates a sense of alignment and thereby safety. They share that experience of alignment and acceptance through connection with others.

The Process: NN4s understand how our pace is part of our wisdom. They move at the speed of emotional knowing. They understand that achieving deep alignment with self takes a process at a meandering pace. As water flows with gravity, so does our awareness of self, always – in the end – finding the deepest place within the body.

Connection: NN4s connect deeply through their lower abdomen to themselves, and then out to the people around them. This creates a sense of deep intimacy, a knowing of others, and an understanding of the emotional content and wisdom contained in the connection.

Skills and Talents

People with NN4 know how to go inside, to what they sometimes call the "infinite universe within". In this deep connection, people of NN4 help others come into alignment with themselves, to feel who they are in the moment. This alignment provides a sense of wellbeing and clarity of self. Their connection to the deep, primal, knowledge of human interconnectedness supports a powerful inner Shaman that some NN4s develop to guide their network of connection. When an NN4 allows their internal wisdom to influence others, magic can happen.

NN4s will talk about "the bubble" – an energetic field that they can expand and place around others to envelop them in the sense of active acceptance and warmth they create when their Natural Number is active. When they include others or a community within this bubble, those within can feel the deep, intimate space created by this connection to self and other.

NN4s help us to feel, process, and understand the wisdom of our emotions. They help us to stay with the emotions long enough to gestate transformation and reach a place of peace and acceptance. Without the NN4 process, emotions can be buried, ignored, or hidden. NN4s help us to learn from our feelings and from the full, internal, bodily experience of those emotions.

Challenges

NN4s aren't as aware of boundaries as some Natural Numbers, and will push themselves to discover how far they are prepared to go, in relationships and in exploring the physical world.

NN4s intimate connections can be misinterpreted as having other meanings than the original intent. People will often interpret it as an invitation into a deeper or more physical relationship. People may consider the person with NN4 to be a much closer friend than the NN4 might think they are.

Because making intimate connections is relatively easy for NN4s, we recommend they make deliberate choices when creating relationships. We often tell our NN4 friends that they should choose someone who "ticks all the boxes", and build the relationship with that chosen one. In all friendships and partnerships, we like to remind them that they don't have to enter into a relationship with everyone. The connection begins to form with others when the lower abdomen is pointed directly at the lower abdomen of another person. A slight offset of the hips creates a break in the connection, reducing the intimacy.

As with so many Natural Numbers, there is a paradox with NN4. With the first phase of activation, people feel a deep sense of acceptance from NN4. Held within the NN4 connection, who we are in this moment, right now, is just fine; yet, we can also feel all the ways in which we are not in alignment, where we are inauthentic with ourselves and our purpose. With this awareness of misalignment, we then begin to question the validity of self-acceptance. If we do not correct the imbalance, we get upset with ourselves, and NN4s will begin to challenge us concerning those exact issues. This can create drama in relationships, either around or with NN4s.

Drama often follows NN4s. This comes from the paradox presented in their complete acceptance of who we are in the moment, combined with the need they generate in others to be authentic. This paradox can create discomfort, especially over longer periods of time. You may at first experience only the warm feeling of acceptance of NN4, and be startled when they recognize and elucidate where you are not in alignment with yourself. This can initially occur energetically, but if an NN4 cares about you, they may directly point out your places of inauthenticity. This can be an upsetting experience if you were not ready to hear and process this information. The added awareness of our emotions that also accompanies the presence of an NN4 may cause some people to react with more passion than they otherwise might.

It is valuable for NN4s to let the people in their lives know that they matter, and to treat the special connections with a little more obvious specialness. This will alleviate resentment and confusion in the love relationships.

Another challenge is conforming to others' ideas of time, and conventions around timeliness. Whatever connection a person with NN4 is in at that moment is the most important connection, and that connection needs to be held and followed to its conclusion. A person with NN4 does not want to end one connection just to satisfy the demands or commitments to the next planned activity. The next connection to be made will need to wait for its time, which will come organically. The person awaiting connection, however, may not understand this process, and therefore become disappointed or feel that they are not as important to the NN4 as the person in their current connection.

NN4s know that time, as others experience it, is a human construct, and not always accurate or of value. While they are aware of the impact of arriving later than planned or requested, their commitment to the connection of the moment takes precedence.

In the Real World: Susan and Natural Number 4s

"When I was learning to activate all the Natural Numbers in my body, NN4 was the first I learned to activate on my own. I had practiced holding the posture with other NN4s, and had a small sense of what the energy of the space of NN4 was like. But, up until this point, I had never been able to release the muscles of my Natural Number 6ness to give over completely and trust that a different part of my body could hold me and offer access to completely new information.

I had been working on this for a couple of days, in community with others who were exploring this process. I decided that I needed some way of keeping my awareness on the muscles of my lower abdomen, while learning to relax all the other muscles in my body. I also knew that I had to be willing to go into my emotions, and through them, to a new place. Up to this point, this concept was purely intellectual – I had no physical experience to understand or compare to my regular experience of life.

We were preparing to listen to the most NN4-inducing music that our teachers had yet found to create the energy and pace of NN4. The plan was to listen to Sheikh Abdul Basit[6], a person with NN4, recite the Quran, for up to 40 minutes – This was not a religious experience, rather an energetic one, using the pace and sound to go deep inside. I had no idea what I was in for.

I lay face down on a mat and placed a tennis ball between my lower abdomen and the mat. Lying on the tennis ball forced me to bring my full

---

[6]Abdul Basit Abdus Samad (Armant; **Egypt**, 1927 – 30 November 1988) was an Egyptian Qari, Sheikh and Imam[2][3][4][5] who won three world Qira'at competitions in the early 1970s and was regarded as one of the best reciters of the Quran in the world.

136

focus to holding my lower abdomen muscles taut so my muscles didn't collapse. I lay this way, breathing in time to the pace of the recitation. I began to use my breath to relax the muscles of my chest, consciously allowing the tension in each muscle to release. At first, I experienced a tremendous fear, and the relaxation of each upper body muscle was met with a frightening sensation: "I might lose control!" I continued, breathing with the chant, slowing my internal pace to a speed I had never experienced before. To me, it felt like time was slowing, disappearing. After some time, I felt my awareness drop fully into the lower body, into the container of my abdomen. I had no sensation of my upper body. My emotions moved to a new place; I was calmer, and my thoughts were no longer triggering new emotions.

First came the warmth of acceptance. I allowed the breath and the chant to take me so deep that I lost awareness of the outside world. This is where my experience became very personal to me. I am telling this story because it was so profound, but this part probably won't happen for you – you will have your own experience.

As I lost awareness of the world outside my body, I began to experience a sensation of being contained within a womb-like structure. I was aware of a beating heart, of warmth and liquid softness containing my body. I was curled into a fetal position (the tennis ball no longer necessary to hold me in this place.) My lower abdomen, my NN4 activation, was holding me there completely.

From here I went through what felt like a full rebirth. My body convulsed and I gave over to a very magical transition back into a new place. As I emerged, I felt myself come back very slowly to the space of the present moment. It took another 30 minutes to begin to feel my body in connection with the outside world. Up to that point, I had only ever lived in the world outside my body, in the energy of the moment. This was my first experience of living inside my being in the infinite space of creation.

This blew me away and changed my understanding of what might be possible for me; was I to find this place of expansion for all of the Natural Numbers? Were they all so incredibly different from my own experience? Did NN4s live like this all the time, with this incredible ability to drop inside and experience a wholly different thing than the present energy?

Was this reproducible? How was it useful? What could I do with this understanding? The questions circled fast and furious. I had already been hooked when I found out my Natural Number 6 power, but this opened so many possibilities for expanding my perceptive and creative abilities. My mind was completely boggled."

Natural Number 4s Interacting with Other Natural Numbers

Some things for NN4s to remember when with people of other Natural Numbers:

1. Most other Natural Numbers are not as comfortable with allowing, paying attention to, or learning from their emotions. Others are more inclined to push feelings down or avoid them. They do not naturally understand the practice of going into the emotions, looking for how they are informing us, and using the body to process the wisdom in the emotions.

2. As a result of the difference in approach to emotions, your invitation to feel and explore them may be met with resentment, avoidance, and/or anger, potentially directed at you. If this happens, dig deeper into the connection and share your feelings – especially any feelings of love and support for the person in anguish. Use your body-based connection with the person to calm and support them.

3. If drama is acting out around you, this suggests that the people you are with are feeling where they are misaligned, out of synch with each other and themselves.

4. After the first sense of connection and acceptance has permeated a community through your presence, the community will prepare for whatever changes are coming through the safety of that connection. The person or community will begin the process of aligning with the truths that have been ignored despite their necessity. Resistance may cause friction. As people shift and

change, they need to establish a new relationship with themselves and each other. You are there to facilitate that process; when you stay in the transition, you enable powerful change to begin and to continue to resolution. If you retract your energy, the transformation may be truncated and incomplete.

5. Often, this process will not feel safe to a person of NN4. In the event that you do not feel safe, evaluate the importance of what is happening, and remember that it is perfectly okay to take yourself out of the experience; you must care for yourself as well as others. If you feel, however, that the transition is too valuable to leave unfinished, search for a way to make the environment safe again for you and the community. This can be especially necessary if you are responsible for the transformation, consciously or unconsciously. If you leave, the possibility for truth and alignment disappears with you.

6. Other Natural Numbers operate at different paces. The body-based Numbers – 2, 4, and 8 – operate at body speed. This can feel very slow when compared with the energy-based speed of Natural Numbers 3, 6, and 9, or the intellectually/spirit-based speed of Natural Numbers 1, 5, and 7. Even the other body-based energies are capable of a quicker pace; Natural Number 2s can match the pace of those they connect with, and Natural Number 8s can act and react with incredible speed when their body signals readiness. These differences in pace are particularly marked in a community, where the other Natural Numbers interact at a different pace. Many NN4s complain that by the time they feel-into what they want to add to a conversation, the discussion has moved on to something completely different. Remember that your perspective is valuable to the discussion, and can still be added. You can actively bring the conversation back around to connect to the earlier subject, or you can use your Natural Number to slow the pace by going inside and taking the community in with you, coming back out with a deeper connection in place. With time, you can continually bring a community back into connection, no matter how challenging the subject.

7. Every connection that you encounter and create is just as important as the next or the last; the connection that is happening now is the one that matters. NN4s stay in the connection until it concludes (or they no longer feel safe); others, when experiencing that connection, do not understand how the relationship can feel so intimate and significant in one moment, and disappear into thin air the next. They do not know where it came from or where it went; they just miss its presence. People may conjure their own answers as to what happened, and few reflect the reality of what has happened. You may be able to help prevent confusion by explaining, in whatever words you feel appropriate, what has occurred, and that the relationship is still important to you.

8. The type of intimacy created in authentic connection can be misconstrued in the world, and is often mistaken for sexual invitation; unfortunately, emotional and sexual intimacy are very confused in Western culture. This occurs especially when NN4s create an intimate connection using their posture of activation through the energetic use of the abdomen. Fortunately, though an NN4's body can intuitively connect with others, making the body-based connection can easily be made a more conscious choice. If you choose not to connect with a person, do not point your hips directly toward them; hold them at an offset angle to avoid the initiation of the more intimate connection.

9. Partner-level relationships for NN4s ares an important choice. You can create such deep relationships with almost anyone. When you find someone that holds that extra level of attraction, let them know that you choose them. They will perceive that your relationships with others also feel intimate. This may confuse or upset them. Make sure that you find ways to let them know that you have chosen them, and that they are special to you.

10. Trust your body sense. If you feel the person that just walked up to you isn't healthy, have faith in your instincts, pull in your bubble, and turn your hips away. It is not your obligation to help every person you meet, nor will you be able to.

11. Sometimes you may need to pull in your bubble, like when you are nervous, angry, or want to protect yourself. People that were in your bubble will feel it shrink away, which may make them agitated and less able to be authentic with you. Again, remember to care for yourself before you care for others – your infinite inner self cannot help a community if it falls out of alignment.

For Those Who Don't Have Natural Number 4

How Others Support Natural Number 4s

Remember that NN4 is about connection – deep, intimate, aligned connection. Learning what this feels like and being willing to dive in can create powerful, deep, authentic, and transformative relationships.

1. If you become visually upset, raise your voice, or lend to a sense of chaos, NN4s may begin to feel unsafe and remove themselves from the situation, energetically, physically, or both. If you want them to continue to be part of the interaction, show them that you and the connection are safe; communicate honestly about the cause of your emotion. You need to put the relationship first as they do.

2. When NN4s end a connection, it is not personal – indeed, the intimacy of the connection may not have been personal to begin with. Recognize that these connections, while intimate, are not sexual or permanent. Learn to enjoy the ephemeral nature of the connection, dive in and explore with the person of NN4 until the connection feels complete, and then let it go. A new, equally interesting and intimate connection will happen next time you meet. If there is any lingering sense of confusion surrounding the intent of the connection, ask for clarification instead of assuming the meaning yourself.

3. Be willing to dive deep into your emotions. NN4s will help you make sense of, process, and extract the wisdom from your

feelings. Ask them to take you deeper, ask them what they see in the connection, and invite them to help you understand.

4. If you find yourself getting upset at what a person with NN4 is saying, look inward first as to why they are they hitting a nerve. What truth are you unwilling to face? Where could you be more aligned and authentic with yourself? Try not to push them away by escalating the power of your response; allow them to take you deeper into the truth, and trust them to see you safely to the other side.

Parenting Natural Number 4

NN4 kids can be very inwardly focused. It is important to support your NN4 child's need to develop a relationship with themselves, and their deep inner world. Remind them to take this time to introspect and examine how they feel about something. Give them space and time to explore; they might love to read, play in their own imaginary world, or spend long periods of time by themselves. Allow them to choose their activities, and if your child is not interested in competitive endeavors, do not push them. When it *is* important that they do something they are resistant to, have a deeper conversation with them about where their reservations are coming from. Check to make sure it feels safe to them. If it doesn't feel safe, they will be reluctant to engage. Be curious about what would make it feel safe to them; try not to override, negate, or ignore their feelings.

Be ready to connect when they approach you to build a relationship. When they do choose to engage, ask questions that reflect how you have listened and are thinking about what they have said; show that you are willing to explore how you feel about it. If you pose a question to your child, be willing to wait for the answer. Listen carefully when they do respond. If you do not agree, share more information about your position and allow your NN4 child to again process their answer with the new information. NN4s operate at the speed of body and emotion. Situations can be processed quickly or − it may seem to other Natural Numbers − ponderously. If you rush NN4s, you will not get an authentic answer, and you may anger them.

Your child may appear shy; shyness in young NN4s is more often an indicator that they are deep inside themselves at that moment and/or they do not feel emotionally safe. NN4s who feel secure will easily come out and make relationships with others. If your child doesn't feel safe with someone, and they have expressed those feelings to you, do not override or ignore their feelings. Check in with your own intuition regarding the person they have expressed reservations about. Be honest in recognizing your own feelings and talk this through with your child.

If your child has a traumatic experience, it is best to address it rather than brush over it. As with any victim of trauma, you will still need to handle the situation as expeditiously as possible but acknowledging the trauma and the feelings will help your child process them. Allow them to express the emotions, and honour those feelings as real and legitimate before you help your child move through them.

In the teen years, it is easy for NN4s to get lost; acceptance disappears on all fronts, and authenticity can be in short supply. If NN4s try to align with others in school without first creating that alignment in and with themselves, they can experience powerful confusion and depression. NN4s report that it can be hard to find their place.

Because NN4s are unbounded in their interior worlds and know we are all one in this place, boundaries in the day-to-day world can confuse them; they may even push the perceived boundaries of their relationships in order to check how strong they are.

It is important to teach your NN4 child about the real-world boundaries of their physical space. Teach them that they create connection from their lower abdomen when they stand directly in front of another person. The connection begins to build as soon as their hips are pointed straight at a person. If they wish to prevent or break a connection that doesn't feel safe or healthy, they should turn their hips offset to the person and break eye contact. This cuts the physical and energetic connection immediately.

Teach your child about their ability to include someone in their energetic bubble. Encourage them to be aware of their bubble, to practice expanding and contracting it so that they become consciously aware of their energetic impact on themselves and others.

Because each connection they engage with in the moment becomes the most important, sometimes they will encounter jealousy or irritation when they put the current connection before their connection with their loved ones. It is important to teach your NN4 child that they are really good at making these intimate connections, so they have to both choose and nurture the ones that are more important.

Teach your child about the difference between their ability to make intimate connections with their body and their sexuality. Explain that this difference may not be clear to others, especially as their peers mature to puberty. They may misconstrue the intimacy an NN4 creates in the connection as an intent to build a stronger and deeper connection than the NN4 actually intended.

When is Activating Natural Number 4 Useful or Helpful?

NN4 is very powerful at helping us find the wisdom in our emotions, to align ourselves with our deeper truth, to draw out our authenticity, and to find our place in the community.

1. When you feel out of alignment with yourself, take time to activate your NN4 center and dive deep. By giving the process the space to work all the way through, you can use your body to enable the wisdom of emotion to come through and bring peace.

2. If you are facing a difficult conversation about something that matters to you and another person or group, consciously bringing NN4 into the moment can keep the group connected. NN4 can help you metabolize the emotions and process that must occur in times of change and transition.

3. If you want to check a decision against your feelings, activating NN4 can help you understand your response. By staying with the physical activation, the energy can guide you through the places where triggered emotions cloud the truth, allowing your body to make sense of their wisdom instead.

4. If you want to bring a community of people together to do something, especially a complicated task that requires people from diverse communities to come together, asking a person with NN4 to help you identify and invite the necessary partners, and then unite the community, can be expeditious and powerful.

Exercise to Gain Awareness of Natural Number 4

Find a quiet place, with a yoga mat or some other comfortable surface.

Option 1: Lie down on your back. Support your legs comfortably with a pillow under your knees, or by keeping your knees bent with feet flat on the floor.

Now, identify your NN4 region: place three fingers on the muscles between the pubic bone and the belly button, the lower portion of the rectus abdominus, also known as the transverse abdominus. Make the muscles under your fingers taut and expanded, keeping your lower core muscles engaged with all your focus on the front of the lower body. Relax the rest of your muscles.

Option 2: Lie face down. Isolate the NN4 muscles of the lower abdomen, making them taut. Find a tennis ball – or other round object that is approximately the same size. Place the ball between your lower abdomen and the floor. Close your eyes and begin your breath where the ball pushes into your lower abdomen.

For Both: Breathe in the world, and breathe out, down into the lower abdomen. Both the inhales and exhales take you deeper inside. Allow the breath to continue initiating in the lower abdomen, continually allowing your focus to drop deeper and deeper down to your lower abdomen. When you breathe in, do not come back up into the upper chest; allow your breath to expand into the lower abdomen instead.

Continue to breathe and stay there for as long as is comfortable. If thoughts and emotions become a barrier, or you find yourself stuck at the chest or upper abdomen, be patient. Just keep breathing and allowing yourself to drop deeper. Imagine that you are a stone dropping through fluid to the deepest part of yourself, all the way to the bottom of the bottomless space.

Natural Number 4 Checklist:

Physical

1. Lead movement with slight hip-forward motion.

2. Blink to go inside frequently.

3. Have softness around the mouth.

4. Have warm, inviting eyes with a watery quality.

5. Are easy to be physically close with.

Nonphysical

1. Know that we have a deep inner world available where we are all connected at the life-force level.

2. Understand that our emotions are an important part of our wisdom and need to be understood.

3. Function at the speed of emotion, and need to know how you feel about something before you can make a decision.

4. Know who needs to be connected to whom and how to establish connections.

5. Drive others to be authentic with themselves in their actions and purpose.

If you identify with Natural Number 4 and would like to verify that this is indeed your Natural Number, visit our website for more information and the next steps on your path: https://bodyof9.com/naturalnumber4

Natural Number 5 (NN5)

Ultimately, everything is knowable and can be understood. Truth is congruent, knowledge is interconnected, and understanding leaps forward when combining intuition, body empathy, and information in a comprehensive framework.

Natural Number 5 Physiology

Body Structure

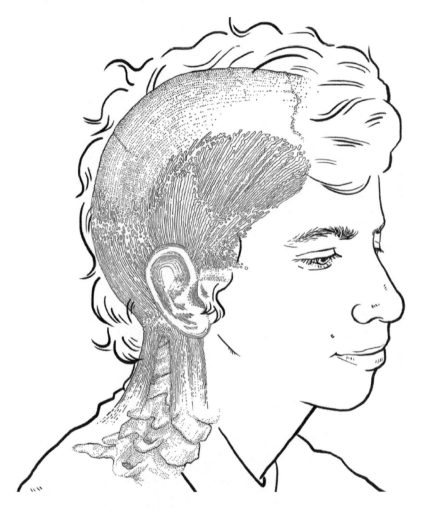

The back of the head, including the parietal bone, the temporalis muscles on the side of the head, and the top of the spine are involved in the activation and balancing of Natural Number 5.

Posture of Activation

People with Natural Number 5 (NN5) create a connection upward from the base of the neck through the crown of the head. The parietal bone of the head demarks the region where activation occurs; muscular activation is created by lifting the temporalis muscles on the side of the skull, elevating the superior temporal line, and creating the sensation of an opening in the crown of the head.

NN5 can be activated using two variations of basic posture; the key in both is extending the spine through the back and upper neck and to activate the muscles that lift the parietal bone.

By standing erect, people with NN5 can draw on the powerful energy above. People with NN5 have a sense of holding the head in space, connected simultaneously to the heavens and to the present. Their bodies are loose and relaxed, as if suspended from the top of the head like a marionette, guiding their movement.

Variation 1: When testing for NN5, we have the person take a wide stance with feet set forward and back, placing their hands on the bent front knee. We instruct them to lower their head down with the neck extended out, while keeping the back flat, straight, and parallel to the ground.

Variation 2: In the alternate posture, the participant stands upright while a facilitator pushes on the hips. The person creates the same sensation, stretching up, lifting at the parietal bone, and consciously pulling energy down into their being through the crown of the head to hold themselves in place.

Facial Structure and Expression of Activation

In the facial structure of NN5s, the upper part of the head is bigger than the lower part, and, in most cases, the skull is large and rounded. The mouth line is straight. The space between the upper lip and nose is wider and has less muscular tone than in other Natural Numbers. The lines that extend from outside of the nostrils angle wide and do not reach the lips as markedly, unless the person is smiling. Very little tone is held in the lower part of the face.

Eye Quality

The eyes of NN5s are round and continuously observing, scanning to take in information; unlike Natural Numbers 1 through 4, the eyes are not looking for – nor used to facilitate – connection. NN5s can actively "turn off" the eyes when they are not receiving input; they may do this when processing information or formulating an answer to a question. Their eyes may roll up and away with a slight backward tilt of the head, or develop a blank, un-present look to allow processing to occur.

Muscular Tone

Most people who embody NN5 have very loose bodies with low muscle tone. When they stand still, you can place your hands on their shoulders and sway them gently; the movement will ripple easily through the body.

Gestures and Movement

NN5s often gesture up into the space above their heads. Their hands are typically floppier and more relaxed than in other Natural Numbers. When they move and dance, it is as though they are suspended in air, supported from above, rather than by the body from below. This gives them a puppet-like, up and down quality to their movement; the loose body tone accentuates the marionette-like quality. They will move their heads often when talking, leading the movement from the back of the head through the top.

Activation and Its Sensations

Creating an active connection out from the top of the head enables NN5s to generate a sense of peace and calm around them. They observe what is occurring around them, without necessarily taking part in the action. Some NN5s have talked about being a player in their own, video game-like reality. They model the behavior of the players, creating an overall understanding of who they are and what they care about.

When people with NN5 are active, they are aware of the body and its sensations as a source of information, but are not very engaged with its physicality; typically, they are more aware of what they characterize as the spiritual body. Some NN5s describe themselves as having an egg-like sphere extending about three or four feet beyond their bodies – their spiritual body is the space between the physical body and that surrounding shell. They are aware of their entire being in this way.

Focus

NN5s have a broad, top-down focus. They are constantly scanning their environment. They are able to hear and, to some extent, follow all that they hear in 360-degrees of awareness around them. Their vision observes and maps everything within the field, and can easily locate specific information. This constant gathering of information, and their innate ability to connect it to their existing knowledge, enables them to hold a top-down framework of their reality, encompassing an understanding and anticipation for the world around them. This empowers others, and frees others to offer their gifts, knowing that the NN5s are compiling and handling the big picture.

Values, Skills, Talents, and Challenges

Core Values for Natural Number 5s

Interconnectedness: NN5s know that all knowledge and experience is interconnected, and can be held in the context of everything that is both known and, as yet, unknown.

Congruence: NN5s look for congruence in what they know and learn. When they receive information that is not congruent, this sets off alarm bells, and the information cannot be added to their map of understanding until – and if – it becomes congruent.

Understanding: NN5s believe that, ultimately, anything can be known, given time and access. This creates a great patience, coupled with a deep curiosity and thirst for knowledge. They are driven to understand both the physical and the nonphysical aspects of our human experience.

Curiosity: NN5s are naturally curious; they are constantly following the breadcrumbs to find the most interesting and relevant information to create new interconnections and leaps of understanding.

Skills and Talents

People with NN5 help others by creating an environment where they can succeed. When people with NN5 make a connection up from the back of the head, they open their awareness to the nonphysical connections of all things. They build dynamic models and maps, using a combination of information gathered from experience, learning, intuition, empathy, and interconnected spiritual awareness.

They are patient and willing to wait for the missing information in their understanding to present itself, or be retrieved from their framework. Using the combination of their knowledge and their intuition, they can make great leaps in their understanding. They use this understanding for guidance, to predict outcomes, and to build possible scenarios. This enables them to help us prepare for the future. They help us to remain aware of what we know and what we don't know, creating a starting point and a direction for forward movement.

NN5s have a sensitive "BS" detector, even if the source of the new information believes what they are saying. When the detector fires, it will take more detailed, consistent, and congruent information before the NN5's framework will accept the data. When presented with new information that *is* congruent with their understanding, they can incorporate it swiftly into their map, adapting their predictions of scenarios and subsequent guidance. They are willing to let go of beliefs to accept better or more accurate data, restructuring the parts of their framework that no longer fit the continuity.

NN5s are able to follow the chains of information in their interconnected web of understanding out to their logical ends, and because they are conscious of what they don't know, they can often organize what they do know to efficiently fill in the gaps. This makes them quick learners, able to take partially formed ideas and extrapolate a complete process through a powerful and well-informed intuition.

NN5 is the starting point for transformation – what are our inputs and resources, what do we need, what is missing, and what are the possible routes to the destination? Once that is in place, we can begin to move forward. As the answers to these questions can shift over time, NN5s may completely re-invent themselves when the moment comes for a change. Some NN5s talk about having a voice, or guide, from which they receive powerful directives. Learning to trust these messages when they arrive is part of the art of NN5.

Challenges

Some NN5s feel meek. When others are behaving aggressively. NN5s are able to connect to the reservoir of power over their heads, their birthright. Through activation and practicing this ability to demand the energy above them, NN5 enable themselves to balance the power dynamic.

NN5s care deeply about fairness and can be deeply upset when one individual is treated with privilege over another. They will work hard to correct the disparity, even at cost to their own health and safety. They may expect, however naively, that others will treat them fairly.

If NN5s don't feel their contribution has been recognized and appreciated, they may become defensive and resentful. If they are challenged about the help they have offered, they may think that they have failed, and feel hurt. They may respond with unexpected condescension or anger. If you detect these emotions in your person with NN5, you or someone else might have hurt their feelings.

When you ask a person with NN5 to take in new information, you may meet with resistance. The level of resistance will depend on the distance of the new information from what they currently understand, combined with the perceived reliability of the source. If you believe something is true, the NN5 will want to know why, where your information comes from, and – most critically – whether it meets the "smell test" of congruence, interconnectedness, and reasonableness. If the source is suspect, emotional, or unreliable, it becomes difficult for them to adjust their framework; otherwise, the framework reorganization is often welcomed.

Sub-divisions exist within the NN5s frameworks. Focused on current projects and circumstances, on which they must spend time to build and curate; NN5s find this is akin to loading information into short-term memory or creating multiple tabs in a browser to leave open for reference. If you interrupt them when they are assembling these sub-scaffolds, the process falls apart and they must start again from scratch. If they were on the verge of an intuitive breakthrough, this insight might disappear forever. As such, interruptions can range from disappointing to devastating for NN5s; they cannot simply pick up where they left off prior to the interruption.

NN5s often don't realize they can ask for help – it is a foreign concept. As they anticipate others' needs, much like Natural Number 2s, they subconsciously expect others to anticipate their own needs, which can lead to frustration when they are not supported accordingly. Anticipating others' needs can also deter NN5s from building relationships with people, as a person represents a particular set of requests and responsibilities for NN5s. If they do not want to take on that set, they will avoid the relationship.

The Story of Martin Fisher, Natural Number 5

For Martin, finding out his Natural Number made sense. Over the course of his life, he had been aware of his nature. In reflecting back on some of the defining moments of his life, Martin shares the story of his journey to understanding – at least at the time of writing this book.

We placed Martin's story of his personal growth in the NN5 section for a number of reasons: first, as Martin is a person with NN5, his story demonstrates how the progression of evolutionary growth is possible when one embraces one's Natural Number. In addition, we are convinced that Body of 9 and its impact would not have been possible without Martin's journey and his reconnection with Susan more than ten years ago. This section therefore contains anecdotes about NN5, but also some 'historical' context for much of the Body of 9 culture.

In the Real World: My Story, by Martin Fisher, NN5

"Welcome to my story – some of the memorable incidents and most defining moments in my life, so far at least.

There is an underlying theme of universal opportunity to my story – the ability to respond to the gifts the universe placed in my way and to notice the sometimes very subtle, sometimes not so subtle, clues revealed to me. It wasn't until I became aware of my NN5-ness that I realized how important and integral noticing gifts and trusting my intuition are to me.

I would like to share some of those defining moments where the noticing and the trust kicked in to create powerful shifts in my life. To paraphrase a radio show from my childhood, "Are you sitting comfortably? Then I'll begin…"

Awakening

My first connection to a nonphysical entity – call it spirit or 'God', as it jokingly referred to itself – was at the age of twelve. My parents, my sister, and I had travelled for a weekend in the spring of 1971 to my grandparents' house in Welwyn Garden City, twenty miles north of London. Their yard (or back garden as the English would say) consisted of a number of flowerbeds connected by sand-colored gravel paths. I would meander along the paths, lost in deep child thoughts during my visits. There was something calming about the energy of the garden.

I still remember the first connection as though it just happened. As I walked the garden path, I heard a quiet but clear voice. It said: "You can always talk to me, at anytime, anywhere," and described a simple, physical gesture to open the connection.

As I reflect back, there was no sense of shock that this voice suddenly spoke to me. I just accepted the revelation that there was, indeed, more – more consciousness, more awareness and, most critically, more unseen. I realized at that moment that I had always assumed there was more – this was my first powerful confirmation of my NN5 connection to that 'more'.

Jumping – The Intuitive Leap

One of the attributes of NN5 is the swift, decisive, and momentous decision-making that can occur. I can recall at least two occasions when an instant decision, that came from some inner place of knowing, resulted in major, positive life changes. Obviously, I have made many other decisions with my more habitual decision-making process, after varying degrees of gathering data from which to decide, with more or less successful outcomes.

One example of making the intuitive leap to a new opportunity was moving to America; I graduated from the University of Manchester in 1980 and started working at a research lab a few miles from my parents' house, to where I had returned after college. One Sunday lunchtime, I was reading the paper and saw an advertisement, complete with a drawing of the Golden Gate Bridge, for a job in Cupertino, California. The required knowledge matched my university course exactly, and I immediately decided to apply, ready to move to America. While it looked like I moved to America based on reading a newspaper advertisement, it was my inner knowing that enabled me to make this decision so immediately.

The Voice

The same voice I'd heard when I was young has nudged me a few times, but the series of events that brought me here to be writing my story depended on my hearing and responding to the voice twice. I truly believe I have been guided here, to find my purpose, to help inform.

The first nudge happened in 2007. My parents had just celebrated their 50th wedding anniversary, and I was in England to celebrate with them. I spent that evening with a friend; we'd gone to the pub at around 6pm and had continued our marathon catching-up session at his apartment. Sometime around 1 in the morning I got a nudge to get in touch with an old friend. The impulse was strong, so I picked up my phone and texted her immediately, just to say "hi." I didn't expect a quick reply as it had been a few years since we'd last connected.

To my surprise, she replied immediately, with bad news. She required a serious surgical procedure. I changed my return plans and went to see her on my way home. Her support group organized a group lunch a day or so before her operation. I was pleased to see Susan (Fisher, to be) there as part of my friend's support team. Susan and I had met working together twelve years previously but had lost touch. I felt a niggling sense of excitement to see her again.

Six months later I called my friend to suggest dinner to celebrate her recovery. She agreed and suggested she bring Susan with her. At the dinner I remember being stunned by how amazing Susan looked, how alive she was, and I am sure I spent more time focusing on Susan than my friend.

It was on my drive home that the voice said very clearly: "Susan said she was ready for a relationship FOUR times." So, I called my friend, got Susan's number (Susan was still in her car driving home), and the rest, as they say, is history.

Well of course...

When Susan identified and formally activated my NN5 in December 2007, my initial response, for a few seconds, was confusion, and then the lightbulb came on. If you watch the video on the Body of 9 website, you can see the sudden spark when the connection is made that validated and expanded my fledgling model of humanity.

I had always known that people weren't the same. From sales seminars, to negotiating practices, and through personal observation, the message that we aren't the same was firmly rooted in my world model. But this explained it all. As I later discovered, this awareness of our differences was likely also fueled by NN5's ability to receive people's inner model, which we NN5s add to our information framework.

My reaction to the truth of the Natural Number identification was similar to that of many other NN5s. "Well, of course." Like any duh! moment, obvious is obvious – once it's been pointed out.

Being Me at Burning Man

Burning Man, a sort of festival held annually in the Mojave Desert, has been an integral part of my transformation and the emergence of Body of 9. The experiences of the 2012, 2013, and 2014 "Burns" will stay with us forever.

One of the "10 Principles of Burning Man" is "Radical Participation," and that, combined with a pretty strong culture of anonymity, means one can be whatever or whomever one desires at Burning Man. I was quite nervous before attending; if I could be whomever I want, who did I want to be? One of the first gifts I received from the experience at Burning Man is the knowledge that who I wanted to be was me! The Playa provides![7] This was another step forward on the journey to trusting myself and the magic around me.

There were other profound lessons from 2012: "Choose Love," "Gifting," "It's Not About You," and the discovery of the broader part of my life's purpose which all came out of that year.

"Choose Love" was the message from a Sunday Choir performance on the Playa and guides us to choose love – not competition, not jealousy, not selfishness – in all interactions with self and others. Choose to love the person and people around you. Cut off in traffic? Choose to love the

[7] Burning Man is set in the Mojave Desert, built out on what is called the Playa. There is a saying: "The Playa Provides," meaning whatever it is you need or are searching for, you will find it on the Playa at Burning Man.

162

driver. It keeps your attitude calmer and more loving of self and other. Adopting this perspective opened me to holding people in a very different light than had become my habit. It opened me to see people from a loving rather than a judging perspective. Without this shift I might never have embraced the fullness of my spiritual gifts.

Another principle of Burning Man is that it's a gift economy. In 2012, the only things one could purchase were coffee and ice. The resulting environment is transaction-less. In a gift economy one doesn't exchange gifts – a gift is just given, with no expectation of a response. Immersing ourselves in this gifting culture was powerfully refreshing.

It became very clear that holding "Choose Love" as a perspective, and offering the Natural Number identification experience as a gift, rather than as a transaction, would be core to the development of Body of 9.

The Free Advice Camp, as our camp was called our first year at Burning man, was anchored by a spinning wheel, with 16 segments. The wheel stayed in service for our entire time at the event, and hundreds of people came by and spun it. People coming by would form a question they wanted answered, and give it a spin, looking for free advice.

The wheel provided an important insight to us as well. 2012 was when Susan started identifying in public, and as more and more people heard about the experience and came to find their 'Superpower', the more excited we became. But we'd go back to the wheel, to check in and see what guidance it would give – and EVERY TIME it would answer 'It's Not About YOU'.

We took this message to heart and hold it still. We are librarians, custodians of this knowledge; it's not 'ours.' Body of 9 doesn't own the awareness of the nine physio-spiritual types. Our job is to raise awareness, to insert this resource back into the world.

My life's purpose had become somewhat visible to me before we'd even left that first year: to bring into the world the awareness that there are nine physiologically different kinds of people. The more focused physio-spiritual component of my life's purpose (to encourage everyone to explore their connection to a non-physical reality as well as a physical one) would not become apparent for a while yet.

Don't Disbelieve

It was in 2014 that I experienced a capability within me, of which I was not previously aware. An ability that made me question my beliefs and led to the "Don't Disbelieve" principle.

My discovery started normally enough. Susan had been working with a woman with Natural Number 9, who had mentioned that she'd injured her shoulder seven or so years before and it had never really healed. I had an urge to see if I could help. From where the urge originated, I don't know, but I try not to ignore these 'nudges,' so I asked her if it would be okay if I worked with her shoulder to see if there was anything I could do.

As I am a Natural Number 5, and therefore somewhat "rules of engagement"-based, it was clear that anything I did had to be nonintrusive (without touching), gentle (both energetically and physically), and in service of the woman I approached. At the same time, I was acutely aware that I knew little about anatomy.

It seemed irrational, but I was pretty sure that there was something I could do.

So, I walked behind her and let my palm move over her back, staying approximately two or three inches away from her, never touching her, just seeing what my hand told my outer self – turning off any brain-processing, just letting my hand scan. I became aware of an image forming in my mind's eye, of a shoulder blade bone covered in scars. Those scars didn't feel physical, rather they felt emotional. I wasn't consciously aware of the image at the time, but it caused me to ask her if she'd had any significant emotional trauma around the time of her accident.

She answered that she'd broken up with her longtime boyfriend the day before her accident. After some quiet discussion in which she realized she had never looked at the connection between the two events, she left the tent, and I didn't expect to see her again.

The next day she returned and said she'd been meditating for much of the previous day and asked me to scan her back again. This time, the hand scan revealed that there were no emotional scars on her shoulder blade, just 'natural' scarring that was already starting to heal. She said her shoulder felt a lot better, but could I scan the rest of her body to see if there were any other issues she could work on. I was skeptical of my abilities, assuming this was a one-off Playa-provided episode, but I agreed.

As I scanned her body by passing my hand over her (as always, not touching her) I felt a weird sensation in my hand when hovering over one of her knees. So, I said, "It feels like a piece of metal here". She replied that she had a steel pin in her knee from a previous injury. I couldn't see her knee through her clothes, and there were no unusual bumps – no other way to have guessed the metal was there. Yet another message that, if I trust myself, I can access information from a non-physical plane to help me here in the physical.

Since then, I've worked with many people, helping highlight body issues, without touching. I have to choose not to disbelieve, as I'm pretty sure I can't believe I can do what I do. But I can, and have done time and time again.

We can't do magic if we disbelieve. Whether this is an NN5 gift, or something more personal to me, when I don't disbelieve, I can do magic, and I'm sure that part is true for us all. We are capable of things we have not yet explored or imagined. Body of 9 is a doorway to this exploration. What that magic looks like – and is able to do, create, and be – is unique to our Natural Number and our willingness to explore, while choosing not to disbelieve. So much more is possible for us than we currently know.

I have also learned that what is obvious to me as an NN5 is certainly not obvious to others who don't share the NN5 physiology. The owning of my gifts, the choice to – at a minimum – not disbelieve, the learning to trust myself and the nudge, and to trust that voice that is willing to tell me "more" about what is possible, continues to open me to a greater fullness of experience. This has been a most exciting time of growth and learning. This validates both me and my abilities and is exploratory – continually opening me to more."

Natural Number 5s Interacting with Other Natural Numbers

Some things for NN5s to remember when with people of other Natural Numbers:

1. Other Natural Numbers are not able to know what they don't know. What they do know is not organized in an interconnected framework of understanding. This means that they will be slower to recall available information, and they may not understand the interconnected nature of something.

2. Other Natural Numbers are more likely to accept information as fact when it comes from a trusted source. They are less likely to

question the source of the information or to dig into the details; this is mostly because they do not have the same kind of framework of understanding against which to check new information. They do not have the same B.S. detector as you – they do not measure new information for congruence with what they already know. This is one way the NN5s help others, by providing a framework to evaluate new information.

3. Reading and sorting through information to reorganize into a more useful format is harder for non-NN5s, and will take them longer to accomplish. They lack the scanning capability and bandwidth of NN5 that allow large chunks of information to be quickly absorbed.

4. You may become impatient when trying to share your understanding with others. This can be because your understanding is congruent, intricately mapped, and the result of years of data collection and organization. You cannot transfer that understanding to others, except the topmost salient summary points. Other Natural Numbers do not have the same mapped context.

5. It is easier sometimes to avoid contact with a person or situation that is difficult to help, rather than dive into a conflict or messy situation. When a person with NN5 is unwilling to engage, they can appear aloof or condescending to others. It is important not to use condescension to keep people away.

6. Your body-reading ability enables you to know how others feel in the moment, though you do not necessarily take on the feelings of others. With the relative exception of Natural Number 2s, others cannot necessarily do the same for you.

7. You are driven to help make things better for others. This ability to provide context, combined with knowing how others feel, enables you to stay calm and remedy a situation for others. They themselves might not have recognized that they are upset or have something that needs addressing.

For Those who Don't Have Natural Number 5

How Others Support Natural Number 5s

Natural Number 5s are about combining their interconnected knowledge with their intuition in order to make leaps of understanding, with the purpose of improving the situation or world as a whole.

1. NN5s will sometimes seem distant. Their existence can sometimes be described as living in a video game – sometimes as a player, sometimes as a spectator, infrequently as the director, and often as the observer. Stepping out of the game into the 'real world' can be hard.

2. NN5s have spent their entire lives building a clear understanding of how their world works. They model the people and environment, which enables them to be very efficient and quick. When the model breaks in some way, they have to restructure – sometimes this means a complete rebuilding, and this takes time. If you notice that NN5s are confused, give them time to reorient to the new information, to fit it into their model or completely reframe it.

3. If NN5s appear to act condescendingly, it is likely that you (or someone else) ignored something they said that was important, and/or hurt their feelings. Look for the underlying cause – it will most likely not be about what they are expressing.

4. If NN5s become frustrated with you, share where you got lost in what they were saying and ask them to lay it out in more detail. If you cannot come to agreement, agree to disagree for now, and table the discussion until more information presents itself. If it feels like they are attached to something, they will likely remain attached until they get new information that would cause them to re-frame their position.

5. NN5s care about things being fair. If you do something for one person, you should do something of equal weight for everyone; it doesn't have to be the same thing. Failing to do so may cost you the trust of NN5s.

6. NN5s love to "follow the breadcrumbs." This means that they love to investigate and apply their curiosity to the things that are interesting to them. Support their curiosity; do not make them feel wrong for taking their time to do the research.

7. NN5s will often talk through a new part of their framework in order to create a deeper understanding. The process of verbally expressing their knowledge assists them in making those intuitive leaps. For non-NN5s, it can feel like the 5s are going on about something they (the non-5s) are not necessarily interested in. Be patient, listen, and add your energy to their process – it will help them with their understanding. Try not to interrupt, as that will break the learning flow.

Parenting a Natural Number 5

NN5 children need to be supported by honouring their differences and calibrating their body-reading skills.

Natural Number 5 children's bodies: Many NN5 children (and adults!) would self-classify as nerds. Some cultures revere nerds; others do not. Especially at school, NN5s may be ridiculed or bullied, and their innate 'meekness' – together with their feeling of watching the video game, rather than being in it – can lead to withdrawal. Helping them become more body aware and self-protective gives NN5 children a sense of confidence in their entity instead of just their intellect. Please note that activities like martial arts, which use an opponent's strength against them, appeal to NN5s' sense of irony. Physical conflict (boxing, especially) can be damaging, as their heads are sensitive.

Natural Number 5s' spirituality: Early on, NN5 children understand there's more than can be seen, but they also know that everything can be known. There's a strong sense of curiosity around how things work (including relationships and group dynamics), and that extends to the metaphysical. Magic, to NN5s, is real, and even though Santa Claus isn't, fairies might well be. Information, not dogma, is important. NN5s will question everything and, as they grow older, will make up their own minds; when they do, take the time to listen to them. The more information they have about any and all spiritual discipline, the more they will fit spirituality into their lives.

Congruence: If you aren't happy, telling an NN5 child that you are happy is a disservice. At a young age they need to know that what they feel to be true in others is accurate. When you withhold information about how you feel it makes it difficult for them to build trust in you, and in themselves.

Consistency and fairness are vital to a young NN5, and even if those traits aren't part of your foremost value system, if you want your NN5 child to continue to respect you as a source of knowledge, they need you to be as consistent as possible.

NN5s have an accurate "B.S. detector", and will remove sources that repeatedly trigger it from the list of trusted references. In other words, it is easy for an NN5 child to lose respect for an adult that keeps setting off their B.S. detector.

NN5s are generally rule followers when they agree that the rules make sense and are applied fairly. Having one rule for them and a different rule for another child will cause significant problems for the NN5 child and may sour their relationship with their sibling, if the rule doesn't make sense and feel fair.

In general, NN5 children get on well with their siblings; they'll look after their younger siblings, but may feel that no one looks after them, even though you, of course, do.

NN5s are continually updating their framework, so logical subjects at school can be fairly easy.

170

NN5 children are self-sufficient and will keep themselves amused fairly easily, especially as soon as they learn to read, as they tend to be voracious readers.

And, finally, NN5 children don't know how to ask for help. Teaching them how to ask for help (and giving it to them or giving an honest answer as to why you're not giving it to them) will serve them well forever.

When is Activating Natural Number 5 Useful or Helpful?

While others will never have the breadth and depth of understanding that comes from a lifetime of gathering and mapping information, the activation of NN5 can help us take a top-down approach. Activating NN5 turns on the impartial observer, enabling you to separate yourself from your environment. It is calming to the mind. The practice of mindfulness was largely designed by NN5s to help us activate our Natural Number 5ness, to quiet our mind, to observe our reality impartially in order to gain understanding and be open to seeing other possibilities for action.

At any point in time, NN5s know where they are and the possible routes available from that point. Activating NN5 in our bodies can calm the mind, enabling us to see more clearly in the moment.

Exercise to Gain Awareness of Natural Number 5

Option 1: Standing with your feet shoulder-width apart, sweep your arms up over head, interlace you fingers, and rotate your palms so they are facing upward. Push your palms toward the sky and allow your body elongate out through the top of your head, stretching the spine. Hold for ten seconds, keeping your body relaxed, and focusing on the muscles on the side of your head to hold you up. Breathe in and allow your arms to swing down as you breathe out. Repeat at least three times.

Option 2: If you have a buddy and a quiet place to lie down, lie down flat on your backs, so that only the crowns of your heads are touching each other. Focus on where your head is touching the top of the other person's head. Allow energy to flow out of your head to your partner, and receive the energy from your partner's head in turn.

Natural Number 5 Checklist:

Physical

1. Relaxed tone in the body.

2. Movement suspended from the top and back of the head.

3. Round, observing eyes.

4. Round head, often with larger cranium than lower part of the head.

Nonphysical

1. Know that everything is ultimately knowable.

2. Experience the river of knowing above the head.

3. Have an excellent "B.S." detector.

4. Look to create understanding and congruence.

5. Have a powerful ability to read the body of others to know what they need.

6. Able to combine intuition and knowledge to make leaps in their understanding.

7. Constantly building a framework to hold, understand, and interconnect their experience, knowledge, and intuition.

If you identify with Natural Number 5 and would like to verify that this is indeed your Natural Number, visit our website for more information and the next steps on your path: https://bodyof9.com/naturalnumber5

Natural Number 6 (NN6)

The aliveness and vibrancy of our human experience is so incredible – stepping into the wholeness of the present moment reveals the energy necessary to create with what is now.

Body Structure

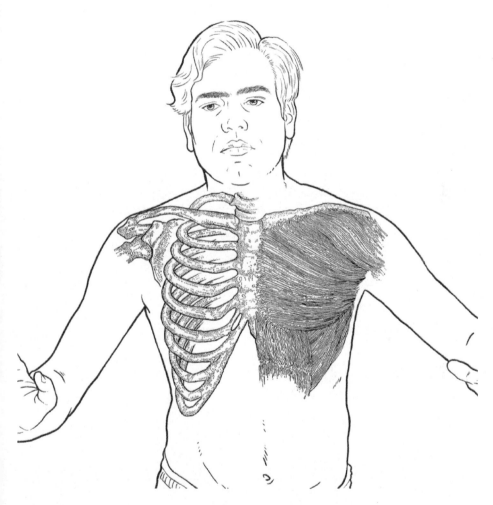

Natural Number 6 (NN6) is centered around the chest, the middle of the sternum and the second to sixth ribs, using the inter-costal muscles to expand the ribcage and chest, creating balance.

Posture of Activation

The sternum, ribcage, diaphragm, intercostal, and pectoral muscles are involved in the activation of Natural Number 6.

To activate Natural Number 6, sit or stand straight, with your head over your shoulders, shoulders over hips, hips over feet. Take a deep breath into your chest, allowing the ribcage to expand as much as possible. As you breathe out, keep the ribcage expanded. Drop the shoulders down and back, lifting more from the sternum. Feel your pectoral and intercostal muscles engage to support the lift and expansion in your chest, further stretching it to a drum-like state.

Notice your awareness expand and your senses heighten. A sense of energetic acuity is created, raising your awareness to the nature of the world around you. It can feel simultaneously peaceful and incredibly alive.

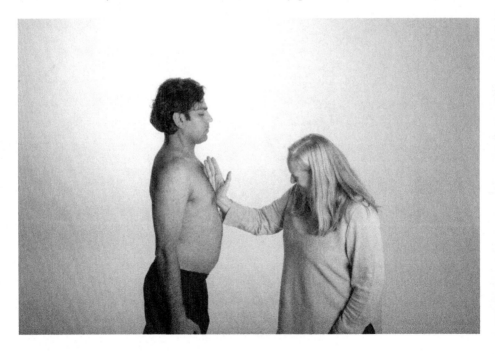

People of Natural Number 6 use the chest like a drum, expanding the ribcage and lifting the center of the sternum, without arching the back or raising the shoulders. The lift is supported with the diaphragm and by tightening the pectoral muscles across the top of the chest; expanding the intercostal muscles fills out the ribcage. This expansion and tension allow the chest to vibrate like a drum, sensing and responding to the energy of the present moment.

NN6s can use the chest to synthesize such energy, making sense of what it means and what is needed; of when, how, and where to move. With the right timing, people of NN6 will share this energy and wisdom to move the community forward on the most alive path.

Facial Structure and Expression of Activation

In the facial structure of NN6s, there is a jowly quality around the mouth where the cheeks puff a bit between the nose and mouth lines. The lips are relatively straight, and NN6s express emotion at the outermost edge of the mouth. Even in a smile, the lip line will remain relatively straight, with the corners of the lips turning up or down.

The NN6 masculine jawline has a distinct turn toward the chin just below the lip line. This is also true in the NN6 female face, but it is often less obvious by comparison.

People often have trouble distinguishing the NN6 facial expression from the Natural Number 8 facial expression. There is no tone or squareness in the jawline of NN6s, and the eyes are alive and responsive rather than resolute and ready, but the biggest facial difference is typically in the cheeks, in the puff or jowl around the lips.

Eye Quality

The eyes of NN6s reflect the alive and responsive quality of their bodies. They are aware of, and readily respond to, that which is most vibrant around them. NN6s don't scan with their eyes and map what they see as a Natural Number 5 would, and there is no particular focus to their gaze until something in the energetic field attracts their attention; if it exhibits interesting, alive energy, then their eyes will focus in that direction to explore the source more deeply.

The eyes of NN6s reflect their energetic and emotional state, ranging from "deer-in-headlights" to "jaguar-ready-to-pounce." When NN6s become overwhelmed, their eyes will take on the quality of preparing to run at any second. When they are near the limit of their patience, their eyes may hold a warning, indicating that if you continue to push them, you may well regret it. When NN6s are relaxed and present, their eyes will take on a loving quality. In this state, NN6s will have the truest read of the current energy, and generate the most aligned responses to what is of service to the community.

Paying attention to the eye quality shifts for NN6s helps you to know what is going on, how they are feeling, and what is likely to happen next.

Muscular Tone

Most people who embody NN6 have high tone in the body. Activating NN6 requires a tremendous amount of tension in the chest, which extends out through all the limbs. This creates a physical responsiveness in the body of NN6s, which enables them to respond to energetic stimuli as soon as they occur.

There is a lifted quality to the chest that makes it look higher and larger than others. Although we might expect that this is caused by the continual expansion of the ribcage over the course of life, this is already visible in the chests of babies and children. The sternum is typically set firmly, and will have no give when pushed on when the chest is activated; the lift of activation also creates a flatter, wider surface at the center of the sternum than you will see with other Natural Numbers.

Gestures and Movement

NN6s gesture out and from the center of the sternum. There is often a power and intensity to their gestures, and the gestures reflect the emotional and energetic quality of where they are in the moment. The arms are typically bent at ninety-degree angles.

All movement for NN6s is connected to the sternum, and centers around the chest. When they are dancing, you will often see them popping the chest up and out, and rotating the shoulders and chest around the sternum.

NN6s are very responsive, and if they relinquish conscious control of the response, their movement can reflect the nuance of the present, or the music they are dancing with; their movement freely expresses the energy of the moment.

Activation and Its Sensations

People with NN6 use the chest to take in the energy surrounding them and decode the content. In this way, the wisdom from the active spiritual energy in the present moment can be shared with others, and transformed into information that helps the world around them move forward. It is a translation of energy into action.

Another way of describing this is that our collective universal consciousness creates collective will; we will call this Universal Will. NN6s can tap into what this Universal Will wants to have happen. At humanity's deepest level, there is a wealth of powerful, positive energy that can be used to create transformation that is desired by, supported by, and in harmony with the Universal Will. By activating the chest and tapping into this energy stream, one can feel the magic and the path for humanity in the body. To make this available to the world around them, NN6s can magnify this energy in its purest form.

When NN6 is activated and their focus is directed at a particular object, that particular object will begin to vibrate with information, separating and sharpening from the backdrop.

Focus

When NN6 is active in the body, there is a sensation of vibrational responsiveness. In this ready state, NN6s feel what is happening around them, wait, and then move into action responding to the energy. Often NN6s will sit at the edges of a group, triangulating evenly around a space and acting as nodes to share the information between other NN6s. They will wait until the energy indicates that something needs to happen, some truth needs to be spoken, or some movement needs to be created. Once something comes alive, they will clarify and amplify it to the group.

With the activation of the NN6 body, NN6s' perceptions — both visual and kinetic — first take in the wider field in front of them, without focus, until the energy invites a more specific focus where the vision separates each thing into its sub-parts to get a deeper understanding of each energy field.

For example, sitting in front of a large computer screen with lots of different windows is at first just a panorama of energy. Through the activation of the chest, something will emerge energetically and then visually from the screen, taking the attention — say it's an image that grabs the focus. NN6s will drill down to understand what, within the image container, is the most interesting and informative. This happens very quickly; the energy and information are gathered in bursts as the focus shifts from the most energetic to the least.

NN6s essentially block information in a field until it becomes relevant. Engrossed in something that is alive, they can close other energy inputs until they have completed the task associated with their focus; they may not hear what someone has said or be aware of what is going on in the room around them. Interruptions that penetrate this energetic exclusion and disrupt their process can be profoundly irritating.

In the Real World: Susan Fisher, Trusting What It Means to Read Energy

"When my kids were small, things would often disappear; usually, it was my keys. They would go missing and a search would ensue. As I think back, I don't think my kids wanted me to leave, but at the time, it became about finding the keys. I had known my NN6ness only for a couple of years at this point. I knew that, if I expanded my chest and trusted the energy sensor, I could feel them, and then I could find them. I started in my living room, expanding and sensing, trying not to think, and especially not to disbelieve.

I could feel the energy of my keys but I was curiously led out of the front door of my house, down the front path to the sidewalk, and along the sidewalk to the edge of the property. The energy said to look in the bushes; I reached in and found my keys perched in the bush. I was completely astounded, relieved, and super happy that I had decided to trust my energetic knowing; otherwise I would never have found those keys in a million years. In my mind, they were somewhere in the house.

Making the choice to believe the power of my body, to be open to new information, enabled an outcome that I couldn't have thought my way into.

Several months later, the keys disappeared again. This time, my middle daughter admitted to having taken them out into the grass field across from our house and somehow, they disappeared. I tried the same approach again, but this time I couldn't feel a thing. We did the normal "look where they were last seen" search, but their energy was completely absent. Those keys never resurfaced! But I didn't spend too much time getting stressed looking for them; I just let them go because I could not feel them at all."

Values, Skills, Talents, and Challenges

Core Values for Natural Number 6:

Significance: NN6s can feel what is true and present in the energy of the moment; this creates a sense of significance. They care deeply about expressing the current moment's wisdom when it is of value to the person or community present.

Aliveness: NN6s feel what is most "alive" in the current energetic space, and will focus on moving it into action. If something is not alive, it is not as interesting to a person of NN6, and often they do not know where to go with it. Aliveness can be a fleeting thing; NN6s are always responding to these changes in energy around them.

Action: NN6s thrive on action. They truly love to do things, and get things done. The sense of accomplishment is very rewarding to people of NN6. When truth and aliveness come together to become significant, NN6s are compelled into action.

What is Next: NN6s are always looking for what is next, and wait in the present moment until they make sense of the energetic answer. This is not about planning for the future; it is about the next response in the next moment, driven by what is currently happening.

Skills and Talents

NN6s are energy beings. They sense the present energy as it shifts and changes, and can know what is happening before others perceive it. They can synthesize this information in order to create a knowing of what is needed next: where does the energy want to go, what does it want to become, and how do we use it to move forward? This enables them to anticipate, shape, and direct the development of what is trying to happen in the moment. They intuitively know what questions to ask, and how to extract the wisdom from the energetic expression of will and knowing.

Once the knowing is clear, people of NN6 share what they have synthesized; they have a way of creating energy and movement, compelling people – and the world – into action. They can amplify and project what they have received and synthesized to help others experience the energy. They are good at summarizing what is occurring in a community for others to see and understand.

Similarly, NN6s are very good at synthesizing group input, offering the alive direction, and energizing people to move toward a goal. They know what to work on next, the order of the actions needed, and what is most alive and important. To distinguish this from the strength of Natural Number 8 in planning and organizing – this is not about looking forward or taking a full view of what is needed. It is about what is next in the moment, right now – going back to the concept of what is most alive and significant. They can be very effective working with or leading teams of people, and produce optimal result when they understand that they need the input from all 9 Natural Numbers. Once the input is understood, they can bring that powerful, manifested energy into any process.

One such important input is love, a powerful force of interaction in this world. When they add love to the process using their amplification power, everything improves. When NN6s learn to use the power of love to create action, the energy aligns for the good of all. This is when NN6 is most effective and appreciated.

Challenges

The central challenge for NN6s is not to allow their responsiveness to spiral into fear and worry[8]. They are very aware of how the energy moves and shifts, where it is unstable and squirrely. If a person with NN6 becomes hypervigilant, this can translate into anxiety. Though these emotions can be offset and quelled by the physical expansion and activation of the chest, the anxiety may also create a vicious cycle in which the Natural Number posture, and the trust in its power, is easily forgotten.

Extroverted NN6s like to talk to make sense of things, and to be sure others have understood what the conversation is about; they will often recap or summarize to be sure everyone is on the same page about what is needed next. Others may become irritated by their need to repeat what has already been said.

At the same time, people may question an NN6's knowing of truth. If the NN6 feels something to be true, it is, no matter what or who is telling them it isn't. *How* they know is part of their gift, and no amount of logical explanation will be as powerful as just speaking the truth that comes from the energy present in the moment. It is important for the NN6 and the community to understand that this sense of knowing is time based – what is true in this moment and alignment may quickly shift with a change in energy, and this is what NN6s are responding to. Repeated attempts at explanations that always fall short of their understanding can be draining for NN6s, and can lead them to losing trust in what they know, diminishing their power.

Another challenge for NN6s is not growing attached to an expectation of what people do with the energy they have offered. When an NN6 gets attached to how their wisdom is received, or if they are looking to create

---

[8] The Enneagram describes 6 as fear-based; while NN6 can go in this direction, we prefer to think of this as responsiveness. When taken to an extreme, it can become hyper-responsiveness. Fear results from being unaware of your true power and nature.

a self-serving outcome, they can misuse their power to redirect and change energy; if their abilities are not used for the benefit of the whole, others have a sense that they have been manipulated, but don't understand exactly what has happened. They can develop resentment toward the NN6, but often attribute it to other issues.

In the Real World: Susan's NN6 Identification

CTI Leadership Program, August 2002

"You are in for a big treat today," said Mike, my leaders' assistant. He wouldn't breathe a word about it, but I could feel the anticipation in his body. As we began each day in our Leadership retreat, the twenty-three of us in the Talkingsticks Tribe were seated in a large circle awaiting the next transformational activity.

A couple named Alan Sheets and Barbara Tovey began to describe what they called New Equations – the name they have given to their discovery of the 9 Natural Numbers. I was intrigued. They invited one of my leadership tribe mates up, explaining what they were going to do. I saw them push oddly on the person, and then tell them something about themselves that seemed to make sense to my tribe mates. I was the sixth person to go up.

Barbara stood in front of me, taking me in. She did some gentle pushes, then she asked me to bring my arms in close by my sides and lift my chest. I liked the feeling as she pushed with more vigorous energy. I felt strong, confident, at ease. She told me I have NN6. (They used different terms, but for the sake of consistency, we will stay with the terms of this book.)

I sat down – but now something was fundamentally different in my body; instead of simply observing my tribe mates being identified, I actually felt something new, like the rush of their souls as they came into alignment in their bodies. With each rush, I was overcome with tears – not tears of sadness or joy, but tears of remembering, tears of relief, and tears of beauty and overwhelming, joy-filled energy. It was as if the floodgates to my soul had been opened to consciously receive the actual flow of energies that were being revealed.

186

Alan came over to me and told me that, if I expanded my chest and met the energy as it came in, I would have an easier time handling and understanding the rush of energy. I took deep breaths, keeping my chest expanded. I noticed that others were not having the same response as I. This blew me away.

Everything in my life that had not made any sense began to click into place. I scanned over the powerful experiences in my life, recognizing how distinctly personal they were to me, and although many of the activities were shared by family members, no one had seemed to be having the same experience as I was. At the time of these experiences, it was difficult for me; I realized my family did not feel what I was feeling. I had been worried that there was something wrong with me, but now, it was all making sense – this is how my body takes in information and experiences my environment.

I scanned the big moments of my past. I remembered my experience at age sixteen in the Jewish Holocaust Museum in Israel. I had become absorbed in the deep, sorrowful energy – the energy of all those lives cut short – and it had felt as if I had been imbued with an urgency and purpose to make my life count. Looking back, I could now see how the energy present in the world around me had indeed informed and shaped my reality and purpose. My family had seemed almost unaffected, and practically ran through the museum. I didn't understand how or why they did that.

I reviewed my teenage experiences of the Cathedrals of Europe, and, as I entered each one, I was filled with the sense of purpose and power contained in the stone walls, pietas, and stained-glass window masterpieces. I saw my family and they were not changed by the flow of information from these seemingly inanimate historical objects. For me, the energy instilled by the creators took over my being, informing me and shaping me.

This information – the explanation of how the physiology of my body worked – gave me a physical way of connecting to my spiritual nature, and a posture in which I could be my most powerful self. I began to understand that my reality was a gift and had a purpose, and that it was magical and important. Being different than my family was a special gift. I was supposed to be that way. Nothing was wrong with me.

My life has never been the same since. That experience sparked the journey I am still on today."

Natural Number 6s Interacting with Other Natural Numbers

Some things for NN6s to remember when with people of other Natural Numbers:

1. Others talk about energy, but do not feel energy in the present as a vibration in the chest. This means their bodies are not as equipped to respond to the present moment. They take longer to feel it, and use different processes to make sense of it, so they may feel extraordinarily slow in comparison to your experience. They may also miss the implications and needed actions associated with the energy.

2. They may not understand the compulsion to act, to move, or to complete, which is a physical drive in the body of NN6s.

3. Other Natural Numbers are not as quick to process experiences because they are not using the reading of energy like NN6s. Energy moves very fast, and the chest of NN6 is equipped to handle that pace. However, the speed can be overwhelming to other Natural Numbers, or to the un-activated NN6.

4. Some Natural Numbers may be more interested in relationships than in getting things done. If this is the case, take some time to connect, look them in the eye, and allow the relationship to develop before you get down to business.

5. Others are not as able or as quick to synthesize energy and information; they may need more time to understand what is obvious to NN6s. Later, others may re-state what you said earlier,

but not acknowledge that you said it. They were not ready to understand what you knew or saw; it did not yet compute. When they do catch up, it feels to them like it was their conclusion, as it landed in whatever way they process. It is helpful to let go of the need for recognition. Does it really matter whose idea it was originally, as long as they eventually get it and get moving? Also, recognize that they may have taken the seed you planted and added their version of fertilizer to the germination – together, you have grown a plant that perhaps neither of you would have ever cultivated alone.

For Those Who Don't Have Natural Number 6

How Others Support Natural Number 6

Remember that NN6 is about aliveness, the movement, and completion.

1. If you get stuck, invite a person of NN6 into conversation about where and how you are stuck. They can help you see where movement is needed, what is alive, and how to start again.

2. If a person with NN6 is getting loud, this means the intensity of the energy in the interaction or situation has risen. Look first at how you might have affected the energy of a situation. If you have brought in lots of tension or emotion, try backing off and allowing the person with NN6 to diffuse.

3. Keep an eye on the energetic state of your person with NN6. What is going on in the eyes? If they are looking intense and dangerous, back off. If they are loving, explore what they are offering. If they are fearful or negative, remind them to expand their chest, and that they are safe in this conversation with you.

4. NN6s are amplifiers of the energy. If you bring big energy toward them, they will return it tenfold, whether loving, fearful,

or angry. It is important to be aware that whatever you give, you will get back magnified.

5. NN6s are alive, loving, and fun to be around when they are feeling positive – encourage their aliveness and positivity. Keep them focused on manifesting positively. When NN6s stay positive, they manifest love and movement. If they begin to manifest anxiety, help them be aware of the change to break the cycle.

6. If NN6s are moving very quickly and you are having trouble keeping up, ask questions to better understand their process and the steps they have left out.

7. In general, NN6s will not respond well if told to slow down or be quiet. It is better to redirect and be curious. They can't help but move.

8. Do not show that you doubt what an NN6 is saying when asking an NN6 to explain why they know something, especially if it is obvious that they feel strongly about it. Again, be curious, especially if it doesn't yet make sense to you. Feel into and trust the underlying truth.

9. If what NN6s have said feels powerful, pay attention. They may not be able to repeat themselves.

10. Provide opportunities to work in groups. NN6s synthesize inputs from the other Natural Numbers to generate new directions; when they operate in a vacuum alone, they can go flat.

11. If you are a coworker or supervisor of an NN6, review priorities regularly to be sure you stay with the energetic shifts. Provide multiple projects, so that if one loses energy, they have something else to work on until it becomes alive again. Interrupt and refocus when they go off track – they may not thank you for it, but they

can understand that in a work environment's schedule you cannot always be working on what is most interesting.

12. Remind them to consider the other people involved in a process or project. Sometimes they can become so focused on completion that they will ignore the details or feelings that could inform them.

13. NN6s are good at summarizing what has happened in a meeting and recapping the action items. In fact, they usually like to do this to be sure that everyone is at the same energetic starting point. In a formal workspace, it can be helpful to directly offer them this job, such that others recognize its importance rather than becoming annoyed with the repetition. In less formal spaces, be supportive of their instinct in whatever manner is available.

Parenting Natural Number 6

NN6 children benefit from lots of activity. They enjoy variety and fast-paced, challenging pursuits. They delight in projects, generally of their choosing, but often prefer not to take those of others, primarily because they have already been started; the exciting beginning and satisfying conclusion of an endeavor are very gratifying for NN6s. Once they have all the inputs, they can work on things independently; however, if they are missing information or materials, it can be hard for them to find that spark and get started. In general, they are most likely to get stuck in the middle of something that loses its energy, and subsequently, their interest.

NN6 kids will focus on what is alive to them and struggle more than most to hold their attention on what is not. Generally, they do very well in school if they are engaged, will learn ravenously about things of interest, and become thoroughly engrossed in their projects. Naturally, there will be times that you must pull them away due to other obligations. Try to let them finish, or find a stopping point where they can easily pick up from later, where they don't have to repeat what they already did in order to get started.

If this is impossible, they may become irritated, especially if they are at a particularly interesting or challenging point of their project. They may feel as though the energy of the process will never be recovered, knowing that the truth of the moment is subject to rapid change. Support them through these emotions such that they can return with positivity at a later time, and increase their chances of manifesting the same aliveness. Similarly, you will need to help them build an endurance to do projects – perhaps schoolwork and/or chores – that do not hold an engaging energy.

When nothing is capturing you child's interest, they will try to create the movement of energy. If they start bugging you for attention, give them something interesting to do that includes a physical component, such as cutting out paper figures, sticker books, coloring, Legos, or play dough:

192

toys that make things. As they grow, teach them skills that enable them to create, such as knitting, sewing, crochet, cooking, baking, sculpting, woodworking, or whatever else they show an interest in. Surprise them with new crafts from time to time; nothing is as interesting as new things to learn and do.

Make starting projects easy by keeping supplies readily available; involve them in figuring out the next step in processes. Give them inputs and nurture their ability to figure out what comes next, and ask questions from time to time to help them learn to articulate their conclusions.

If they are stuck, they may not know what they need to get moving again. Sometimes it takes more inputs or conversation; get curious about where they are stuck, start asking questions, listen to their process, and bring your piece of wisdom in. In other instances, it just takes time. They may become impatient and uncomfortable waiting; teach them to sit with those emotions until things feel right to start again.

If your child wants to try something and there is good reason not to – danger, expense, etc. – ask them what they think will happen if they continue; make a game out of figuring out the chain of causality; include silly predictions to keep the mood light, make sure they put the pieces together in the end, giving them a sense of agency in the outcome. Don't play on fear or anxiety; this may paralyze their ability to make decisions, rather than empowering them to make informed ones.

NN6 kids are full of energy; they want to play and do things with others. In groups, they enjoy working effectively with their peers, and will take to leading or participating depending on what is needed in the energy of the dynamic. They require the input from all the other Natural Numbers in order to do their part in full – helping to figure out what comes next. Often, they will sit quietly and take in what is going on, until it is time for action. Once they know what is needed, they will move into the place of leadership and create the energy needed for movement.

However, while being liked and included in the group is nice, it's not as important as being respected and listened to when they have important information; they will want their ideas and their guidance to be heard and acted on immediately. If they are not heard, or feel that things are moving too slowly, they will raise their volume. Raising volume is very easy for NN6s because the chest expands like a drum, causing their voices to carry and resonate. This can be alarming to the others, and their peers and teachers may criticize them for being too loud.

Be clear to your child that you honour their ability to be loud and fast, moving at the speed and intensity of energy; simultaneously, teach them about their impact, and to honour the pace of others as well. Help them to find and be comfortable with different volumes and speeds; this is something NN6 kids can learn, but they will need guidance and practice. Varying speed and volume can be framed as a fun game, which will help them to develop a value for others' process without making them feel wrong for what comes naturally.

To help your child not to be fearful of the world, teach them how to lift and expand their chest when things become overwhelming. In their expanded posture, they will be able to make sense of what is happening. If they start to get overexcited, invite them to take a deep breath, and take it with them. Encourage them to use the breath to expand their chest, and find the enjoyment in relaxation. Say things like, "Wow, we are getting pretty excited! So much fun! Let's take a deep breath and enjoy that feeling! Phew!" Avoid phrases like, "calm down", "slow down", or "quiet down"; they don't know how, and they are likely to grow angry and resentful. Teach them through your own actions and impact on the energy – they learn new skills best through your example.

Remember that everything is a body/energy experience to your child; an announcement of a need is very urgent to them. Pay attention to the physical cues of your NN6 child. When they are expanded in the chest, relaxed in the rest of the body, and aware in their facial expression, they are likely doing well. If you see their expression take on a "deer-in-headlights" or "jaguar-ready-to-pounce" expression, it means they are no longer centered and they are at risk of running away or blowing up – the latter occurs when the energy around them cannot be processed and builds dangerously in their body to the point of explosion. If they are in this state, try not to push them; send them loving energy, offer a gentle touch, take a deep breath with them, and give them time to figure out what they feel or need. Be aware of the circumstances that can cause such overstimulation. When there is too much energy, chaos, or noise in a

194

space, it can be hard to for NN6 kids to make sense of what is happening. If you can, remove them from the overwhelming situation to somewhere they can have a quiet moment to recover.

Your child, especially when young, has no idea how they make other people feel; without faulting their instincts, teach them about their impact. In most cases, NN6 children never want to hurt or displease someone willfully, but sometimes the compulsion to see what happens when they push the energy in a particular direction can be too enticing. Teach them to be aware of how easy it is for them to change course, to shift the direction of energy and intent. Acknowledge when they do this. If they do something that has an unpleasant consequence, ask them to consider the impact and whether they would like it if you did that to them. If they say yes, and the action will not harm them, ask permission to do it, and follow through.

Deal with the transgression in the present. If they go quickly from mischievous to contrite, with or without your guidance, acknowledge the change and praise them for it – don't hold a grudge and punish them for what happened in the past. They will not understand why something that has passed is being held as more important than the present.

NN6 kids love in a very big way! Acknowledge that love and encourage using that love in what they do.

They will magnify whatever energy they receive – recognize that what they show you may be a reflection of your present energy, or what was available in the space. Teach them to be aware of their energy level and its source.

NN6s do well in competition but, ultimately, competition will make them anxious; repeated victory may also make them obnoxious. Teach them that it is more rewarding when everyone is included; this is especially true with siblings. NN6 children who are younger siblings do not perceive any difference between themselves and their older sibling, and may dislike that others think there is a difference. Help them find their own identity separate from their siblings. Don't compare them, and, in general, don't praise the older sibling in front of them; find another time for that praise. When you do this, you provide a path for competition describing exactly what they must do to show you there is no difference between them and the older sibling. When they achieve what their older sibling has done, and don't receive like praise and recognition, they may grow resentful.

In the Real World: Susan's Comments on the impact of fear and shame for Natural Number 6

"I hear a lot about how NN6s can be perceived as fearful. I see it as hyper-awareness that can become hypervigilance. It is important to acknowledge your NN6s' awareness as real and help them to breathe into it to feel if it is safe or not. When the worry overcomes the truth, NN6s lose track. Acknowledging their concerns is important; they are real, and they feel them. To deny them is to deny the power of their NN6 sensor. This can cause them to lose trust in their internal compass, their sense of truth that comes through the chest into their being.

NN6s do like to talk. I catch myself telling every little detail, especially when talking with my mother who has always listened really well; I will tell her every little detail. There is something in the saying of the experience that helps a person with NN6 to make sense of it, to weed out the truth from the experience, to enjoy the aliveness of the experience, and to explore and find what is next. NN6s also learn from the conversation.

I do think NN6s get shamed for their speed, their volume, and their energy level. "Too" is the descriptor that often goes in front of the shaming words – too loud, too fast, too much. NN6 is a powerful force; help them own it and understand how to apply it so they don't get shamed into smallness. The good news is that, for the most part, NN6s don't suffer as much from shaming, unless they convert it into fear – *fear* of being too loud, too fast, too much. Then they can shut down and try to disappear.

My mother, NN1, sometimes used shame to try to control me. For the most part it didn't work very well. But there were some big messages that she gave me when I was young that I think did handicap my development, particularly around the being too much, too visible, too

196

talkative, too "self-absorbed". I think the talking is misunderstood as being "all about me" (which sometimes it is, so we have to watch that). But often it is just about what the person with NN6 has synthesized from the moment, what they need to share in order to move the world forward. Sometimes there is a compulsion to tell everyone what is needed next, what something means, and what to do about it. Helping NN6s to understand the importance of timing, and how good they are at knowing the right timing of things, is really helpful.

Also, because NN6s are able to manifest things from the energy, when they manifest for their own benefit, it can feel manipulative and selfish to others. They do not necessarily realize how they have manipulated the energy to get their way. They also don't realize how others are not able to do what they can do. This was something my mother would shame me about, when she felt that I wasn't compassionate or considerate enough of others.

Teaching NN6s about their power to manifest is also really important. NN6s think that everyone can do that. It is a special gift, which makes NN6s really productive, but puts pressure on them to keep performing. Honour this incredible ability to create and keep going. If it gets shut down, everything will grind to a halt."

When is Activating Natural Number 6 Useful or Helpful?

NN6 is extraordinarily useful when you are feeling stuck, need to make a decision, or want to make a list of prioritized actions. If you do not know where to start, or what is needed next, adding the activation of NN6 to any experience can gain a clearer sense of the alive direction.

If you want to manifest a particular reality or vision, bring NN6 into the process; this will help bring the energy of manifestation.

NN6 combines well with Natural Number 3 and 9 to accelerate and clarify a transformation. Natural Number 9 brings the expanded reality, the bigger context, and the breadth of what needs to be considered. NN6 narrows the attention to the container in which the effect can manifest, and Natural Number 3 focuses and accelerates the energy of manifestation even more clearly and specifically.

Exercise to Gain Awareness of Natural Number 6

Stand facing the wall and place your palms against it, arms in an L-shape, with elbows pulled in tight to your sides. Take a deep breath and expand your chest, keeping the chest expanded even as you breathe out. Roll your shoulders back and down so they are at rest. With your weight on your back leg, using it as a post, push the wall, meeting the energy of the wall through your whole chest, keeping your arms and chest taught and connected in tone, and focusing on the lift from the center of your sternum. Notice if your awareness shifts. Push for three to five seconds, then release and repeat five or six times, taking time in between each push to make sense of the energy and any shifts. You are practicing expanding your chest, maintaining tone, and feeling with the drum of the ribcage and intercostal muscles to read the energy.

Natural Number 6 Check List:

Physical

1. Can expand the ribcage and lift the sternum.Has a larger/higher, more expanded ribcage

2. Has movement centred around and lead from the sternum.

3. Has vibrant, aware eyes.

4. Has jowly, rounded quality to the cheeks around the mouth.

Nonphysical

1. Responds at the speed of energy.

2. Magnifies energy back to others.

3. Knows how to move a person or a community forward.

4. Works with and synthesizes the input of all to know the most alive direction.

5. Shares what is true or alive in the moment.

6. Lives in the present with awareness of what is happening right now.

If you identify with Natural Number 6 and would like to verify that this is indeed your Natural Number, visit our website for more information and the next steps on your path: https://bodyof9.com/naturalnumber6

Natural Number 7 (NN7)

To open to the possibilities that are still unknown is to create space for profound change. To care deeply about the possibilities for the world to be its best creates space for that change to happen.

Natural Number 7 Physiology

Body Structure

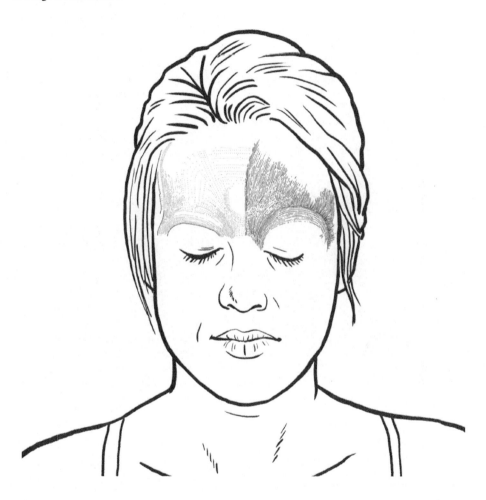

Movement for Natural Number 7 (NN7) is centered around the forehead, including the glabella – a small flat bone in the middle of the forehead above the brow – the sphenoid, and the frontalis muscles.

Posture of Activation

People with NN7 straighten and lock the back leg. The chin is dropped down and tucked in toward the throat. The whole body leans forward in activation. There is a straight line moving down from the forehead through the body to the back heel. Focus is brought to the third-eye area, the frontalis muscles and the glabella. NN7s experience a quieting of the mind, opening to stillness, and enter the infinite realm of a dream space where the ideas, images, and visions can be received through the third-eye area. In this space, they can witness a multitude of possibilities. They may envision all kinds of permutations on an idea, and sense what needs to change for the world or the people around them to live and be better. As they return with their new understanding, they will present it to us as a possible truth for consideration.

Facial Structure and Expression of Activation

NN7s move into a waiting state where they are very still, receiving information. They have an attractive, ethereal quality that makes us want to wait with them to find out what they know.

In the facial structure of NN7s, when active, you see a more prominent third-eye area at the glabella, the flat bone at the centerline of the forehead just above the brow. The eyebrows and mouth are fairly straight. The chin tucks down and in, and the forehead gives a sense of moving forward. When active, the expression can feel distant and unavailable.

Eye Quality

The eyes of NN7s have an infinite quality; a sense of possibility, mystery, and knowing is held in their gaze when they are activated, no matter the age of the person. It lends to the mysterious and attractive quality of the NN7.

It is not always clear that they are looking at you, or taking you in. This is one of the ways that NN7s are misunderstood. When absorbed in the infinite connection they are able to establish, NN7s can seem unavailable. Until they share it, others find it hard to discern what occurs behind the infinite eyes.

The NN7s' center of activation is also known as the "third eye"; some report seeing better with the third eye than their "little eyes."

Muscular Tone

In contrast to the other Natural Numbers, the tone, shape, and hold of NN7s can be varied, and appears to depend more on if or how they choose to explore the limits of their bodies. One thing that is consistent is their tendency, when standing, to put one leg back behind their body and lock out the knee for stability.

Gestures and Movement

NN7s lead their movement from the brow or third-eye area. They punctuate their expressions and words using their forehead, and have a variety of interesting ways of moving their head to illustrate their meaning. They will often point from their forehead with their arm, hand, and fingers.

They are extraordinarily creative with their movement, sometimes in their own world, sometimes with you. Their movement is often hard to match and follow, and doesn't necessarily follow the same beat in the music that others are tuned into.

Activation and Its Sensations

When NN7 is active, the body is sensed as the vessel of existence. Paolo Scoglio, NN7 described it as follows:

"This is a process. It begins with a quieting, then a gradual opening. The focus on the third eye must be sustained for the infinite realm to begin to be sensed. It is in that opening to the infinite realm that the sense of a dream space begins to appear. I conceive of it as a black hole in the field of vision that begins to include patches of other colors. Eventually a bluish purple (indigo) color emerges as predominant and the black hole expands. In this expansion a shimmering golden ring appears at the edge of the hole. In times of the deepest meditation the black hole (turned indigo) takes over the entire field of vision in the third eye and the golden ring is the boundary between this dream space and the external reality. This can all disappear in an instant, as the light of worldly reality reappears.

The body is like the golden ring. The consciousness of the body gets greater and greater as I go deeper into 7. The body begins to tingle slightly in the way the golden ring shimmers around the opening. Activation generates a simultaneous consciousness of the inner world and the outer world."

When learning to cultivate NN7 in the body, it can be more effective to start with the eyes closed, bringing focus to creating tension in the frontalis muscles in the forehead, and dropping the head forward while tucking the chin in and down. Under closed lids, the eyes can look up toward the third-eye area.

For non-NN7s, the activation can be disorienting, as the awareness of the body can disappear, and anyone who has not yet cultivated a relationship with the infinite may find the empty space disquieting. Once the experience is understood, people talk about reaching the still-point, the waiting space that can precede a journey into the as-yet-unknown reality.

Some NN7s enjoy and create guided meditations. They are able to follow the path through the infinite to a new awareness, realization, and possibility. When not actively cultivating the infinite, NN7s are full of ideas and possibilities. Using this active imagination, they are able to entertain themselves. Often they will spend more time with their awareness in an alternate reality of potentiality than they do in the present moment. More experienced NN7s recommend those newer to their activation consciously remember to check back into the present, bringing their ideas and possibilities into their bodies.

While NN7s are capable of traveling out of the body, this can leave their physical form vulnerable, and make getting back to the present moment more difficult; it also inhibits the simultaneous consciousness mentioned earlier. This is the reason for coaching NN7s to let the universe come to them; going out creates the disconnection from the body.

Focus

When NN7 is active in the body, the focus is not primarily on the here and now; it is open to ideas, possibilities, and new ways of being. This can take many forms, ranging from playful to admonishing. NN7s use all that

206

is at their disposal to help their wisdom to land and be heard in the present moment, moving others in the direction of their vision.

The attention of an NN7 is an interesting challenge to observe. When the possibilities are still presenting themselves and the core vision has not surfaced, NN7s can move between concepts at a rapid rate; others perceive this as a lack of focus. NN7s tend to think out loud, and each of their thoughts seems important as if they are pronouncements. These seemingly important pronouncements begin to sound conflicting when held together, but for an NN7, the thoughts are separate elements on the path toward an ultimate conclusion, decision, or statement. When the vision and goal become clear, NN7s have an amazing way of creating a community focus and determining the processes to get something done efficiently.

In the Real World: Sophia, an NN 7 Child

"I will tell a story about a Natural Number 7 child I knew. This illustrates the profound challenges that young NN7s face when growing up in our world. I will call the child Sophia for the purposes of this story.

When Sophia was about seven years old, she began to explore her passion for reading. She read everything she could get her hands on and developed a fascination for stories with mystical plot lines. She began to read books at higher reading levels and with more grown-up and sophisticated plots. Sophia was becoming intrigued and expanding and developing her imagination.

As she got deeply into the books, she would lose herself in the worlds presented, imagining herself sharing the experiences of the characters in her books.

At the same time, her awareness that she was different from other kids was beginning to burgeon. Her first spiritual awareness was poking its head into her reality. Up until now she had used her inventiveness to come up with creative and fun games to play, and to entertain herself when school was boring.

She began to read the Lemony Snicket books, *A Series of Unfortunate Events*, which are about a fantastical reality with magical, sinister characters and young children being preyed upon by evil forces. As she read these books, the reality she conjured from the images became more real to her than the reality she was in at the moment. She became supremely frightened, unattached from the normal feeling of safety provided by her room and family. She was in a total panic.

Her sisters knew she was more upset than normal and summoned her mother, who fortunately knew that her daughter had NN7. She called a good friend who shared NN7 and asked what to do. It was clear that her daughter had left her body, and entered her imagination so fully that she wasn't in touch with what was going on around her. There happened to be two Natural Number 8 friends spending the night, and her older sister also had Natural Number 8. The mother's NN7 friend said she should have the Natural Number 8s lie on her, to cover her windows with blankets, keep the lights on, and help her begin to feel her body through touch and containment. Once the sense of safety and containment was created, it took about an hour for Sophia to calm down and feel her body again.

Understanding the degree to which her child's imagination operated her reality was a powerful experience for her mother. How it impacted her child's sense of reality was, when she was honest with herself, a bit frightening. Understanding a bit more about her daughter's NN7ness helped it to make more sense.

Without this knowledge, and the advice of her NN7 friend, her first response would have been to take her daughter to the hospital. With this option, she would have been drugged and sedated, neither of which would have helped her to learn to recover her relationship with her body.

Developing the ability to recover into the current reality, to hold open the possibility for the expansiveness of reality available to NN7, and keep it tethered here, is a skill that NN7s need to develop.

Also, as a parent, Sophia's mother realized she had to monitor and pay attention to the books her daughter used to explore her reality. No more Lemony Snicket books until she could manage this herself."

Values, Skills, Talents, and Challenges

Core Values for Natural Number 7:

Freedom: People with NN7 value freedom for themselves and others – the freedom to experience adventure, to open to where vision, curiosity, and intuition can take you into the unexplored. This may show up as a resistance to boundaries, status quo, and rules.

Fun and Adventure: Fun and adventure are staples to people with NN7. The experience of exploring their world can be highly entertaining. In that space, they can be very adaptable to the ideas and possibilities that present themselves.

Possibility: People with NN7 value staying open to possibility, exploring different directions, and seeing where curiosity leads. They help us stay receptive to possibilities that have not yet entered the realm of the known.

Truth: NN7s need to know it is safe to be honest with you, and they want you to be honest with them. They don't need or want a sugar coating of truth; they want to be able to tell you how they see things in the present moment.

Skills and Talents

NN7s are liminal beings that help us grow and change. Through their imaginative inner consciousness and connection to other possibilities, they generously and vulnerably offer us information that they perceive we need in the here and now. Often, they see what needs to be released, expanded, or shifted in our perspective of our life experiences and beliefs. Approaching this as a lens of adventure keeps us open to change and willing to explore. Through curiosity and fun, they invite us into the transformation process.

By showing us how much they care, allowing us to see their vulnerability through their passion for the vision they are offering, they can build trust, and help others to trust change. This passion they have for transition, reconstruction, and transformation makes it easier for us to move through the life-death cycle. The image of the Phoenix rising up again from within the flames of death is called to mind – something has to die, be destroyed, or be released to make space for something new.

NN7s have coined a term for their method of evaluation called the "Utilitarian Calculus". It is an assessment that consists of four essential questions which are weighted depending on the NN7's perception of the situation and its importance. They ask these questions unconsciously or consciously of themselves, their projects, other people, ideas, or imaginings:

1. Is it good for the world?

2. Is it good for me?

3. Is it the right thing and best thing for me to do?

4. Am I doing my best?

Our NN7 community has told us that everything is constantly being evaluated through their own weighted version of these questions.

This Utilitarian Calculus is part of what enables NN7s to change, to help us change, and to keep the community focused on the possibilities. This is a constant dance for them. NN7s are always moving us toward an elusive future, one which they see is possible, but which we may not yet perceive. Their challenge is to make this future visible and enticing, such that the other Natural Numbers will bring together their gifts to manifest this vision.

There is an enigmatically attractive quality to NN7s, a sense that they know something we would like to know. We are attracted to the mystery, energy, and excitement they can exude. They use this magnetism to bring us together.

There can also be a feeling of "danger" that tends to accompany the presence – if not the invitation – of the unknown; we do not know what is about to be revealed. We might sense that they are going to call us out, to ask us to be better than we are being and stretch beyond where we are now. Sometimes we need to be brave when approaching them.

Challenges

The endless stream of possibilities can freeze NN7s. Combining this with losing connection to their bodies and environment can prove challenging to recover from without support in their lives.

"Existential Dread" may be familiar to all people, but can be particularly devastating to NN7, and can occur if a path that had answered "yes" for all questions in the Utilitarian Calculus suddenly changes to "no." Existential Dread is described by NN7s as a frozen state where they realize that what they have been doing, the person they have been with, or a path they have been followings, no longer meets the criteria of their Utilitarian Calculus. This can create a feeling of pointlessness and futility –

that what they are doing or where they are focusing doesn't matter. If allowed to spiral, this leads to feelings of depression and stagnation. They cannot see how to start again.

Finding a sense of purpose can be very important to NN7s. For many, this comes in the form of service, where they can easily observe that their actions make a difference to someone. However, when they identify with any path, practice, discipline, profession, or relationship that later becomes suspect, shame may overtake them. This can happen over and over again for an NN7s until they recognize that their NN7 gifts, strengths, and way of existing in the world offers consistent meaning, even if the apparent source of meaning is subject to change.

When in the state of existential dread, NN7s tell us that the way out is to just pick one thing that they can do next. Taking a single step forward, then another, and another, can create the movement needed to overcome the emotions of dread, futility, shame and disappointment. With practice and support, NN7s can come to trust in their being; that their purpose and interests may change over time, and they will need to accept that change to learn, realign, and move forward.

NN7s' gift is particularly valuable when brought into a community where it can be understood, used, and manifested. In order for their vision to be received, they need to be in connection with the people in their world. When the connection is missing, NN7s can feel extraordinarily lonely. They can feel as if they aren't heard, and that it is unsafe to bring their wisdom forward.

NN7s begin delivering hard-to-hear messages to others from a very young age – messages about how we can grow and change. If they are ignored or met with resentment, "corrected" for the way they deliver their wisdom, they begin to distrust themselves and others.

Throughout their lives, NN7s are constantly challenging the rules and boundaries laid down around them, pointing out where ideas have ceased to be useful, or are actively inefficient. In order to bring new information into the world, they cannot be bound by existing structures – those may need to fall in any case, to make way for change. Others use boundaries for protection, interaction, or rules of engagement. NN7s see them as restricting possibility. As a result, they are constantly challenging limits, testing the reality that is presented to them by others and tearing down what fails to hold water. They are conscious that the rules can and should change over time; they may even envision variations of reality in which a boundary has already ceased to apply. Sometimes the status quo must be shaken to bring in new movement.

This is often and misinterpreted as selfishness or recalcitrance by people of other Natural Numbers; they may view the constant challenging of their rules and reality as disrespectful, disruptive, or manipulative. This misunderstanding happens most frequently when NN7s do not establish connection with others before bringing forth the challenge. Learning the importance of connection through showing their honest vulnerability and depth of care is an important skill for NN7s to develop.

In the Real World: Susan and Natural Number 7s

"The initial activation of NN7 came easily to me. The posture, the energy, and the way of being were familiar. One of my daughters has NN7. As a Natural Number 6 (one of the side numbers to NN7), I had always understood her, seen her vulnerability, and held it as vitally important to support the unique way of being that came with her NN7ness.

But I had no idea how to get to the depth of openness, the full-on experience of NN7, and use this power without the body-awareness that comes with my Natural Number 6.

One of my colleagues, an NN7, decided to help me. There were also two Natural Number 8s who were there to hold space for my experience. The colleague with NN7 put me in the posture of activation, and she held me in the posture while activating her NN7 as powerfully as she could. I had never held the posture with the activation this powerful or for this long.

Up to this point, I had backed out of the activation just as it began, not waiting for the true magic to happen. This initial activation was sufficient for me to be strong in the posture, but not yet strong enough to access this space at will for my own experience. It was enticing, but the new and different intensity presented at the edges of my reality were a bit daunting.

This time was completely different than any prior experience. As I stayed in the NN7 posture, it felt like I was losing connection with my body. Up to that point in my life, I had never let go of my bodily sensations. This time I allowed myself to find a new way to use my body, from the forehead! It was as if I was suspended in air from my forehead. I saw purple energy that took the form of an eye. It disappeared and an infinite universe, free of thought, replaced my normal reality; magical, infinite space surrounded my awareness.

It was a truly incredible feeling to allow myself to float in this infinite space, to feel the limitless possibility, and the beauty and majesty of this space. My world is normally so bounded in the present moment, so full of the aliveness of the energy present in the moment. In comparison to this unbounded freedom, the completely foreign reality of NN7, I was awed and profoundly changed.

As I returned to my physical state, after standing in the 7 posture (in a darkened room) for fifteen to twenty minutes, I nearly fell over. I was caught by the two Natural Number 8s that were holding the tether to the earth for my experience. It was a very good thing that they were there, not just because I would have fallen over, but also because I had to find a new relationship to my body and the world around me upon my return. Their solidity and connection to the earth and to the body assisted with my re-entry. I could barely speak for an hour or so after the experience.

This was my second experience of moving so deeply into the energetic reality of a full-on activation of a Natural Number other than my own. In juxtaposition with the first time I had an experience of this magnitude, with NN4, I began to understand the fundamental difference and importance of the function that each Natural Number performs in creating a sense of wholeness and understanding of our human experience. I understood at a metaphysical level the importance of having access to all these possibilities. This was a new and vitally exciting territory."

Natural Number 7s Interacting with Other Natural Numbers

Some things for NN7s to remember when with people of other Natural Numbers:

1. Other Natural Numbers do not see the possibilities that you see, and in fact they may not be interested in all of the possibilities. Have them help you sort and prioritize your ideas; invite them to help you see what to do next, and choose an option.

2. NN7s will often ask a lot of people their opinions. This is not to be convinced of a particular option, but rather to be sure they have considered all the perspectives involved.

3. Others use boundaries to protect themselves. When NN7s do not respect these boundaries as they challenge them, others can get confused, scared, and resistant. If you know that you are going to push a boundary, give the person who will be affected a warning, and explain why this is important for you to do.

4. It may not be obvious to others how much NN7s love and care about them and the world. When you let people see this with honesty and vulnerability, it helps them understand how and why you do what you do. If others don't know your depth of caring, your actions may seem detached from reality.

5. When you feel that your involvement in something is done, even if the project is not completed according to others' definitions, allow yourself to move on. Allow the other Natural Numbers to take the responsibility to finish the project. Be sure you have held the vision long enough that the project is not derailed on the way to completion, but do not allow others to pressure you into staying involved beyond the point of usefulness, especially when it damages your sense of efficiency.

6. Being a successful NN7 requires mustering a level of vulnerability, truth, and an expanding capacity to connect with others. Your vision is not accomplished in a vacuum from the other Natural Numbers. You are the catalyst to create the community and hold the vision for others.

7. Other Natural Numbers are not capable of envisioning that which is obvious to you about what needs to change, die, or move on. Speak what you see, but do not attach to what others do with what you present! They have heard you, but may not be ready to engage.

8. NN7s need friends that are loyal, honest, and stable. They typically will make a few friends that last a lifetime.

9. NN7s need a nest where they can build a calm, familiar environment. This is a safe place for them to recover in once they have been out in the world creating.

For Those Who Don't Have Natural Number 7

How Others Support Natural Number 7s

Remember that NN7 is about possibility, growth, change, and moving toward our greatest purpose. NN7s will hold you responsible for moving toward being your best self. They will tell you the truth of how they see things.

1. Remember that you may not recognize how deeply NN7s care about you. Signs of vulnerability, irritation, or insistence on you seeing what needs to change are signs that they care. Look to the deeper feelings that underlie the actions.

2. Ask NN7s what they are thinking about and listen without judgement as they tell you. Marvel at their imagination. They appreciate being asked, heard, and seen.

3. Ask NN7s how you can help. They may hesitate in allowing you to help because they may not be comfortable with collaboration, or might not trust that you really want to help. Conversely, tell them directly how they can help you – they will enjoy the concrete and actionable purpose.

4. Be careful when assuming the reason for their behavior; ask them directly what moved them to do something, and what was motivating the behavior. Refrain from judgments until you understand their position.

5. NN7s may keep asking for something, even after you have said no several times. They are looking for where the boundaries lie, and then when they find them, exploring their purpose. What is this boundary really? Where does the boundary hold as a truth in reality? Where does it fail? When the boundaries are perceived by NN7s as unclear, limiting, unfair, or inappropriate, it is an opportunity to move in a new direction. It is a process of checking for what is important – to you and to them. If you plan to say "no" and hold firm, do it early in the discussion and make clear that the issue is not up for argument at present. If you have said "no" for some other reason – more time or more information – state what you need to explore new options.

6. It may be hard to intuit what is important to an NN7. In one moment, it may seem like the thing they are asking for is the most necessary thing in the world to them, and that there will be devastating consequences if they do not get what they want. However, if you hold the "no" position, they will grouse for a moment, and then let it go completely. Other times, they may seem to care little for a request which turns out later to be tremendously important to them. They may feel bitterly

disappointed that you did not see and understand. It is very important to ask them directly how important something is.

7. NN7s can struggle with existential dread and depression. They may not be able to identify the source of their feelings. Support them through these emotions, and encourage them to choose one thing they can do to get going again, then another, step by step. Once they overcome the inertia and are moving again, they can find their way.

8. NN7s may do or say things that can be shocking to others. Sometimes this is expressly to shake up your perspective or open you to another point of view. Sometimes it is an exploration of possibility: can we go in this other direction? Once they learn to recognize and follow the rules of engagement that exist, NN7s will better understand the value of courtesy and observing others' feelings. Even then, they will at times challenge these limits and rock the boat a bit. Evaluate what they say and do, with this understanding taken into account, before you judge their actions or words.

In the Real World: Paolo Scoglio, Natural Number 7

"Susan Fisher, Morten Nygård, and I all had similar identification experiences. The concept of the Body of 9 was an important part of the Coaches Training Institute (CTI) leadership program through 2003. Accessing inner strength was fundamental to this CTI training. They engaged vendors with expertise in helping individuals access their inner strength in various ways. As soon as I was identified as a 7 by the vendors known as New Equations, my curiosity was piqued. When a person was led to find their effortless strength, it was as if their hearts opened, and light and wonder poured out of them into those witnessing the revelation. The successive pulses of energy became almost overwhelming. With each revelation in the other individuals I became more and more full of a sense of the profound. After witnessing twenty-two other people be identified, I could barely contain my curiosity and interest. At the end of the process I asked to join New Equations' training program.

I entered that training early in 2003 and there I met Susan, the author of this book. We trained together for nine years. Then Susan began exploring and developing a new understanding of the physiology and manifestation of the Body of 9 beyond the original concepts introduced by New Equations. Over the next four years I followed Susan's work. Being intrigued with her discoveries, I reconnected with her in 2016 and decided to study and work with Susan and Martin, to continue to develop the practices and understanding of the Natural Numbers, and to affiliate with her organization, Body of 9.

Transformation

Learning how to accentuate my NN7ness gradually and steadily transformed my life. A process of re-examination, ongoing learning, and the addition of new practices changed my life and my professional work. For me, as an NN7, it was a process of learning how to be more and more embodied over time, more present with others and in the moment, more aware and oriented to the fabric of relational connection and personal significance.

The understanding that there are nine different kinds of people, and consequently nine different perspectives, and nine different interpretations of reality, moved my professional practice in a new and more rewarding direction. I became a more effective life/leadership coach and psychotherapist. I could connect with clients more readily, understand their worldview more quickly, negotiate the alliances with greater agility, and more quickly connect with positivity and disconnect from negativity.

It had been my practice, every four years or so, to learn a new modality or specialty, to keep my work fresh and interesting to me. Since learning about the nine Natural Numbers, I haven't had the same need to learn a new modality. I am constantly learning through the context of Body of 9; it continues to be an ongoing way to keep things fresh and interesting for years now, and I expect it to continue.

Benefits

Since being identified and learning to activate all nine Natural Numbers in my body, accessing my innate strengths and gifts is easier. There is less effort, greater trust, more peace, and an expanded sense of love and appreciation for others and for life itself. There is an open path of discovery when the nine ways of being are understood and integrated.

Conflicts and misunderstandings are understandably inevitable without knowledge of the nine ways of being human. This knowledge is not a simple solution. It is, however, the best solution I have encountered for disconnecting from fears around others and being misunderstood by others. It is the best solution for managing stress, anger, rage, hostility, racism, and xenophobia. Embedded in this solution are nine paths, nine ways. The magic of this solution is that one of the paths will resonate with each person and will begin to generate alignment in each individual who embarks on a learning path.

Learning to embody all nine of the Natural Numbers seems to be an inevitable path for humanity. I see the ubiquitous understanding of the Body of 9 becoming a global truth that will transform many social norms and social structures for the good.

Appreciating and Enjoying Susan Bennett Fisher

Susan is an inspiration. Her ever flowing fountain of enthusiasm for exploring, learning, understanding, teaching, and writing about the Natural Numbers in the human body, and building the Body of 9 organization with her husband Martin, is amazing to watch and be a part of.

Susan is gracious in her way with me. She has been so generous in being willing to bring me up to speed with her expanding knowledge of Body of 9. She and Martin have been inclusive and collaborative with others and myself around the creation of training opportunities and building the Body of 9 organization.

Susan has a big heart. She feels like a sister as well as a friend. She has included me in her family over the years. She and Martin have been open with their home and Susan is always readily available to me to answer questions or just ponder the nature of being.

My friendship with Susan has grown over the years. I have always seen her as a dedicated mother and intensely enthusiastic about the Body of 9. She has always been open, generous, interested, attentive, trusting, and playful with me. Over time I have seen her be more clear in vision, driven and self-directed. Her qualities have been and remain compelling and inspirational for me. Susan's enthusiasm for understanding the physiology of the nine Natural Numbers has moved her to create a teaching organization and write two books about the subject. I continue to learn from Susan as she uncovers more of the telling details about the differences in the nine physiologies associated with the Natural Numbers. In the midst of all this creation, and from the identification process, Susan has expanded her capacity for slowing down, for listening more intently to others, and for communicating with people of all nine Natural Numbers."

Parenting Natural Number 7s

Parenting NN7s requires some different rules and support than other Natural Numbers. Realize that as a parent, you do not share your child's experience of life; some of the aspects of support that your child needs may feel like they are in conflict with your personal beliefs and core ways of being.

NN7 children start to test boundaries very young, because they live in an un-bounded reality. They will challenge rules, ask questions, and push the limits they encounter to "try on" different ways of being. Help them understand the purpose of the boundaries that you plan to hold. If you are clear and consistent from the beginning, they are more likely to respect them, and incorporate them into their own sense of reality. Working with your child to develop boundaries can be a revealing experience, and will cultivate a trusting relationship. Ultimately, they may find a few reliable structures in their life to provide a touchstone of relaxation when their heightened sensitivity to physical and metaphysical stimuli begin to overwhelm.

Your NN7 child will begin giving you feedback and messages about how you can be a better parent, soon after they begin to talk. Listen for the truth in what they say. If you get defensive or irritated with what they have said, there is an important underlying message for you to explore.

Keep in mind that the feedback offered by NN7 children is not about disrespect – it is about finding the smoothest, most efficient solutions for everyone, where all needs are met. They may speak their mind to improve communication, or as a way of feeling for trust, measured by how the people close to them react to their wisdom. If you refuse to listen to them due to irritation or disbelief, they will have a difficult time trusting you as a parent. In the end, it is more important to them that you have heard them, than that you agree.

As they grow, teach them about the rules of engagement, and how they can be used to deliver information and messages more effectively. Emphasize that their instincts and contributions are valuable, and that employing some rules will help their messages land. Explain that others do not see the possibilities, perspectives and solutions that are obvious to them, and as a result they may interpret the solutions they present as being solely for the benefit of the NN7.

Generally, NN7s only follow rules that they feel are concrete and defined. Be sure that your rules are built on sound logic, and hold the boundaries carefully. Be clear to your NN7s that there are consequences for transgression, whether they think those consequences should apply to them or not. Bear in mind that sometimes a negative outcome may be worth the experience for them.

As your NN7 child grows, they may become resistant to direct requests for them to do something, such as household chores, errands, or other mundane contributions. It can be powerful to engage them in designing their contribution to the family, and help them experience the purpose and value of teamwork. They do very well when they feel that they are being of service to the community. Set a timeframe for them to do it "in their own time". They may be processing something and will complete it when they are done. In addition, notice and acknowledge when they make a contribution without being asked.

NN7 children may ask for things simply to see if they can get them; often it is not clear whether something is important to them or not. If you are inclined to give the requested item to them, do it right away, or tell them the exact circumstances under which they will get their wish. If you never intend to give it to them, let them know that right away, and don't change your mind.

Sometimes it may seem as if something is vitally important to them, but once you have held the boundary, they let it go as if it didn't matter at all. Have a method that you agree on with your NN7 child to determine how important something is to them. For example, if your NN7 child is motivated by money, ask them if they will pay for part of what they are requesting. This request helps them to figure out how much it is worth to them, why there is a connection to it, or what possibility it creates for them. This kind of request facilitates learning and discernment, and can build the confidence to interact more intricately with life.

Sometimes, it's not about having things, but rather about having the experience of having those things. When the experience associated with those things is over, it's over, and the item may become superfluous.

NN7 children need a nest. Often, they will naturally keep their room orderly and comfortable. Help them to design their space in a way that supports them and makes them feel safe, somewhere where they can retreat to regroup and process. Giving clear ownership of things and space, with a choice to share it or not, will build trust.

Because NN7 children are not as embodied or tethered to the moment, it is important that you teach your child about their ability to access other dimensions without leaving their body. Help them develop ways to keep attached to the physical as they begin to explore their NN7 abilities. This can become very important around age seven or eight as they start to cultivate their spiritual being. Encourage them to daydream when they are processing, and to practice mindfulness of the present moment.

NN7s can focus well on something when they are interested; once they lose that interest, it becomes very difficult for them to continue a project to completion. They will change direction frequently; they might become interested in a sport, invest the time and energy to reach a competitive level, and one day they wake up with no interest in playing again. Trust that they have likely considered the many potential consequences of their decision using the Utilitarian Calculus, and allow them to shift and change when they are ready, unless there are specific ramifications of their decision of which they are unaware. They are here for possibility and need variety to be able to pull connections together. The process is more important than the performance.

NN7s begin to explore with curiosity all aspects of their being. Encourage their curiosity. Ask them what they are thinking about. Marvel at their ideas and help them make choices. Entertain possibilities and focus less on right or wrong. It's important to explore for the sake of exploration; to this end, encourage daydreaming, storytelling, and projects without a purpose.

They may bring up subjects that don't seem age-appropriate – conversations around death, religion, or whatever profound subjects they are exploring. Be willing to engage and talk openly with your NN7 child on any topic in which they are interested.

224

NN7 children need loyal and trustworthy friends; often they prefer to have a small group of friends sustained over time. It is important to help your child cultivate their relationships with their chosen few. The parents of your child's friend will not necessarily understand your child's behavior, especially in comparison with their own children. It is important that you talk with these other parents to explain how you support your child and how that might be very different from their child. If you become curious and align with the other parents, this will help your child maintain the relationships that are important to them. Talk with other parents about how and why the friendship between your children is important.

Your NN7 child is much more vulnerable than is obvious. The infinite quality of their eyes can make them difficult to read. Look beyond what is on the surface, and watch their behavior. The sensitivity to other realms can make the physical world feel very abrupt and shocking. Overreaction or shutdown can occur when they feel over stimulated. Depression in the teen years is not uncommon. NN7s have an innate understanding of the impermanence of life and can experience existence as pointless. When they get drawn into this awareness, they can lose their connection to their sense of value and meaning. Guide your NN7s to finding their purpose and look for ways to be of service; they do best when they know they are helping people they care about.

NN7s kids care deeply about others. This caring is often misunderstood, especially when it comes out as a message that someone is not ready to hear. As they are able to see different possibilities or outcomes, it is difficult for them not to worry and care. People often interpret the motivations of NN7s as selfish; this is rarely the case, as the improvements and possibilities are mostly focused on the community or the world. Their ability to envision a better way might be couched in terms of how they would benefit, but this is not their core intention.

If a child with NN7 chooses to tell you something, and they are met with resistance or derision, they may shut down or become angry and resentful. When this occurs repeatedly from multiple sources, they may come to distrust their instinct to give information freely. Most NN7s feel that others do not listen to them. For young NN7s, it is important to let them know you heard their message; acknowledge their ideas, and coach them on how to present their wisdom in ways that allow others to hear it.

Be aware that siblings of the NN7 child will notice the difference in the rules you are applying. You might seem too willing to bend or change the rules for the NN7 child. Have honest conversations about why each child gets different rules, discipline, and support.

In the Real World: Penni Blythe's Response to Parenting Natural Number 7s

"Your NN7 child will have been giving clues way before they could talk. A quick shift of the head, a struggle if they feel too tightly held, distress if touch isn't definite (but not heavy). Being held back, being told "no" as their fingers, eyes, mouth explore everything in sight, while difficult to avoid doing as a parent, can confuse the permission needed around their natural curiosity. Despair, whining, and dissociation need noting and attention. Don't just distract them to divert behavior; they will need an explanation for the distraction. And never say, "Don't cry…"

On the subject of boundaries – if you let firm boundaries drop, they will see it as a betrayal and a lack of trust will set in. Boundaries must be felt to be fair and flexible. Allow them to question and discuss them so that they can identify what is and isn't negotiable, and why. "Why" is one of the most crucial words in the NN7 lexicon. I vividly remember my mother screeching: "Why do you have to ask so many questions?" and me replying, almost instantly, "Because I have to." Understanding your reasons helps them accept the boundaries.

Please, please avoid phrases like "sit still and stop wriggling," "Pay attention," or "Look me in the eye when I am speaking to you." NN7s do not need to be looking at you when you speak in order to hear you; in fact, it might distract them from what you are saying. Rather, use phrases like: "Oh, what do you see/hear/feel…" Approaching them with your curiosity active is important. Telling does not work. Engaging, inviting design and exploration about how and why are very helpful.

They can quickly feel hurt and disengage; they may withdraw if their offerings and spontaneous contributions are not acknowledged. Also, inauthentic praise is ineffective. Be authentic and honest about where you are or you will lose credibility with your NN7.

When assisting them in designing their nest, invite them to choose colors and textures – how things feel is very important to them. Believe them when they tell of ideas, or things they see/hear/feel that seem "out of this world" to you or others. These things are real to them. With respect to dreams, NN7s often have no distinction between dreaming and the real world. To an NN7, they are just different and equal dimensions of existence. Encourage your child's exploration of their metaphysical self.

With respect to focus, yes, yes, yes! Their focus is second to none when engaged. When it's done, it's done. Please don't say things like, "You never finish anything." They complete what was needed; it is not necessarily their job to finish it in the way that you would. Also, they can appear to make a decision completely out of the blue. This is not the case; their processing is so fast, in ways that no one else sees, so to others it may seem sudden or not thought through.

It is so true that our motivations get questioned and misunderstood all the time. I remember on numerous occasions being told that I was doing something for "my ego" or "my benefit." This cut me to the quick – it truly wasn't so and led to much heartache and pain. It truly is important to let NN7s know they have been heard, to acknowledge their ideas, coach them on how to present their wisdom in ways that others can understand. Use phrases like, "Tell me more about that…"

NN7s really want and appreciate fairness, and can be hurt and angry when rules seem unfair and inconsistent. Be really truthful, and explain why things are different. "This is why X got this and you got something else." This is crucial in developing trust with your NN7."

When is Activating Natural Number 7 Useful or Helpful?

For people of other Natural Numbers who learn how to create the activation of NN7, there are certain times and applications where it is very useful.

1. When you want to create a complete change in your life, in order to find a new direction or purpose, activating your NN7 and/or engaging an NN7 in your process will shed light in a new way.

2. If you are facing a mystery that you do not understand, or a situation that is confusing or confounding, opening to the infinite through your third eye – activating your NN7 – may give access to new information that will help you move forward or understand what is happening.

3. If you are stuck – not able to move intellectually, emotionally, spiritually, or physically – NN7 energy can un-stick you.

4. If you want to create a community around a vision, involve NN7 to help build the community and hold the vision; this will make the community more powerful and directed.

5. If you want to improve a process, make something more efficient, or find a new way to do something, NN7 is excellent at making a difference.

Exercise to Gain Awareness of Natural Number 7

Find an open space on a wall. With arms straight, palms flat on the wall, position your body as if you are pushing into and supported by the wall. Straighten the back leg, locking out the knee. Bend the front leg comfortably, being sure to have enough space between the legs to get a full back-leg extension. Drop and tuck your chin toward your throat.

Close your eyes. Bring your focus to the center of the forehead at the eyebrow line – your third-eye area. While they are still closed, roll your eyes up to look at the third eye. Stay in this position for as long as is comfortable – the goal is to create stillness in your head and being, to open for new information to come in. A place of complete emptiness may occur that can be confusing at first. Stay with it until something new starts to happen.

Natural Number 7 Checklist:

Physical

1. Prominent brow with flat glabella.

2. Infinite, unreadable quality to the eyes.

3. Tendency to stand with one leg back and locked out.

4. Tendency to lead movement and gesture with the forehead.

Nonphysical

1. Value freedom and curiosity.

2. Explore possibility and change.

3. Care deeply about the world.

4. Function best when of service.

If you identify with Natural Number 7 and would like to verify that this is indeed your Natural Number, visit our website for more information and the next steps on your path: https://bodyof9.com/naturalnumber7

Natural Number 8 (NN8)

To know life through the body and the body's connection to the earth is to know how to build and create with power, gentleness, and integrity for the good of all.

Body Structure

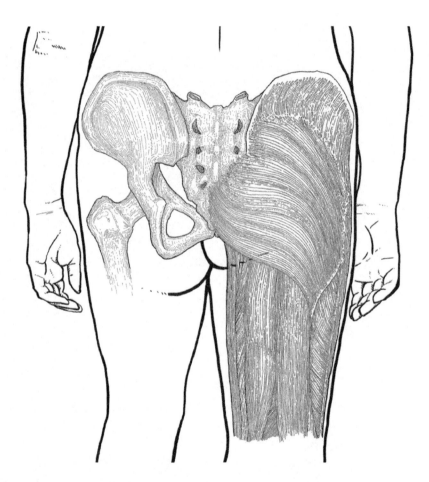

The movement center for Natural Number 8 (NN8) is centered around lower back, including the sacrum, supported down through the legs into the ground.

Posture of Activation

NN8s connect down to the earth from the sacrum through the gluteal and hamstring muscles. This creates a posterior tilt of the pelvis, a flattening of the lower back and a tension in the abdominal muscles around the middle of the abdomen. This stacks the spine to allow the upper body to sit relaxed and balanced on the sacrum.

The energy travels down from the sacrum, through the legs and feet into the ground, using the earth as the base of a powerfully balanced triangle. The energy travels down and up again in a bi-directional flow. It can feel as though the feet grow roots into the earth. Everything goes through the body, creating a feeling of balanced power in the base triangle and relaxed ease in the upper body.

The posture helps NN8s to balance their energy, preparing to meet the world square-on so that, no matter what comes, they are ready for action. The posture energizes all the cells of their body. They become highly aware of all aspects of their bodily functions, sensations, and physical experiences.

Facial Structure and Expression of Activation

In the facial structure of NN8s you see a strong, set, resolute jawline. The lips are set in a firm straight line that has a pursed quality to the hold. The eyes match the jawline and lip line in their power and readiness. The cheeks are very even, and don't puff up in any significant way.

Do not misunderstand this expression. They are not angry, distant, unavailable, or other emotional descriptors that might be associated with this expression in someone who does not have NN8. This is a beautiful expression of their natural power, their ease with their bodies, and their readiness for life.

Eye Quality

The eyes of NN8s are resolute and ready, taking in the situation in front of them. When interacting with another person, NN8s can make direct eye contact, but they do not necessarily build or form relationships through it. They can offer reassurance, a feeling of safety and trust. They are reading you with their eyes to see if you are present and trustworthy in the moment, checking to see how aware you are of yourself and of them.

Muscular Tone

Most people who embody NN8 have high tone in the lower body and a more relaxed, gentle tone in the upper body. The lower body muscles involved in the activation are strong and powerful, giving a grounded feeling to the body. They are very gentle in their touch, aware of the impact their body has on yours. While they appreciate a good strong hug and solid contact, it must be given with gentleness; they model this gentleness in the way they hug and acknowledge others.

Gestures and Movement

NN8s are grounded to the earth. Their gestures are typically powerful, often using a fist moving down in a directed movement. When they walk or move, their feet barely leave the ground, and they often lead more down and backwards than forward, from their sacrum, when dancing. Sometimes they will rock the upper body on the sacrum. All the movement is led and centered from their low back/sacral area leading to a sense of solidity down through the legs to the ground, even in movement.

Activation and Its Sensations

When NN8s are active, they are ready to respond proactively; they know the series of actions needed to make something happen, what must be taken care of, how to take a good idea and create the reality. The sensation of power and preparedness in the body gives a feeling of assuredness – "I am ready to handle anything."

Either standing or sitting, bring your focus to the small of your back; tilt the sacrum so it points downward toward the ground, and clench the gluteal muscles in your buttocks. Feel the energy extend down through your legs to the ground, as if you are pushing into the ground. It might feel as if your feet grow roots into the earth. Allow your upper body and jaw to relax. The torso is perched and relaxed on the sacrum. This posture creates a deeper awareness of your body, its connection to the earth, and the flow of energy up and down.

When NN8 is active in the body, the energy is grounded and powerful. There is a balance between power and gentleness that can be both comforting and confusing to others. When NN8s are in action – taking care of someone in an emergency, for example – one can feel this balance manifest in a sense of safety.

Focus

Because the body of NN8s is so alive, at the cellular level, inside the body, the outside world feels still to them. Their bodies are continually sending

236

signals to their awareness of what is happening in their surroundings. The more in-tune with these signals an NN8 is, the more quickly they are able to respond, especially in an emergency. Their focus is rooted in their body.

Through their bodies, they understand and respect natural human boundaries. This is reflected in one version of their posture of activation: arms-length away, until invited closer. They teach respect and body integrity – how to listen to our bodies and follow where they guide, how to create safety, attend to the critical details, and move when ready. As a result of this body readiness, they are able to respond quickly in a crisis situation and are often the first ones to move into action when needed. On the other hand, if their body is not ready for change, they can be reluctant to make a commitment or give an answer. They are constantly receiving information from what they energetically sense through their physicality, and using that sensed information to move forward.

In the Real World: Susan, Carol, and a Deer

"I was once sitting around a table with a group of people having lunch outdoors on a beautiful day. We were chatting and enjoying being out in nature. Suddenly Carol, NN8, rose from the table and sprinted off, running up the steep hillside at break-neck speed. Ahead of her we could see bounding animals. A few minutes later Carol returned to the table, barely winded but her body still on high alert.

We all stared at her incredulously. What was all that about? Carol said to us: "I saw the deer and her baby approaching the steep slope and the barbed wire fence. I was worried they would not see the fence and get injured, so I decided to steer them away from the dangerous area."

The rest of us realized that: 1) we hadn't seen the deer; 2) we would never have noticed the fence; 3) if we had seen the deer and the fence, then we wouldn't have made the connection to the danger; 4) if we had made the connection to the danger, we would not have responded; and 5) if we had responded, we would never have bounded off up the hill in the manner that Carol did, and it would have taken conversation and a plan to figure out what to do.

Carol, in her NN8ness, simply allowed her body to take over and respond to what it perceived was a dangerous situation for the animals.

This can happen for NN8 in any situation that is dangerous to any being. Her body told her exactly what to do and knew what she was capable of doing."

Values, Skills, Talents, and Challenges

Core Values for Natural Number 8:

Trust: NN8s value trust. There are three parts of what trust means for NN8s: 1) they need to feel trusted by others, giving them a sense of purpose and value; 2) in relationships, trust means that all people take responsibility for their part of the process, i.e. say what they will do and do what they say; and 3) there is also the component of trusting their body and listening to the wisdom it provides.

Loyalty: NN8s value loyalty in all meaningful relationships. Loyalty grows out of the relationship, as trust builds. NN8s are loyal as a part of friendship. This shows up as a strong feeling of support or allegiance for people they trust.

Integrity in the Body: For NN8s, everything goes through the body. Because of their hyper-awareness of the body, sensations and feelings inform them of what is going on, what is important and, if needed, what should be done. They know that they need to pay attention to what their body signals.

Skills and Talents

People with NN8 have a body-based understanding of what to do, when to do it, who needs to be involved, and how to execute for optimal results. They have a strong, physical sense of what is right and wrong in the moment, and how it will affect the future. Throughout life, this awareness becomes shaped by experiences into a personal integrity that informs their actions and decisions (often this is not something others would include in a definition of integrity).

When applied at the level of the community, the sense becomes focused on managing the best measure and means for accomplishing the goal. They tend to be capable planners and facilitators. When they feel a project is flowing and progressing well, with all participants taking responsibility for their part, they drive and empower the community's actions. If they perceive that the community is not taking enough responsibility in the process, or is executing it without integrity, they may take charge and do most of the work themselves to assure that it is done correctly. When they trust the wisdom inside their body, they are able to lead us forward with integrity.

NN8s will hold others accountable for living in alignment with their personal integrity; this comes down to meaning what you say, and doing as you promise. If, for instance, you claim to be a vegan despite occasionally eating meat, they will question your personal integrity and lose trust in you. This judgment is not about whether you should or should not consume animal products – it's that you have taught them that you can't be taken at your own word. While this example may not be important enough to many NN8s to make or break a relationship, it will factor into how they view your reliability.

Their earth rooted power and body-based wisdom give them a special relationship with nature and animals. They have an internal drive to protect and care for the planet, and all beings on it. Their instinctive ability to care for animals, when nurtured, is a source of wellbeing for themselves and the creatures in their charge. They will often treat their animals as well as, or better than, their humans.

When at home in their bodies, they are at home in the world around them. Their ease and power, and their comfortable sense of self, is very reassuring to others. When NN8s are not in a place of ease with their bodies, everyone around them feels this. When NN8s are upset, feel threatened, or are not able to create a sense of safety with their bodies, the possibility for that atmosphere of security disappears in the community.

They have a built-in sense of what is safe, as if their body has an early warning system through their connection to the earth. When they trust this body-knowing, they are able to avoid danger and keep others safe. This does not mean that they will not engage in what others consider high-risk activities, such as riding motorcycles, bungee jumping, or sky diving; when their body signals that they are safe, NN8s can fully enjoy the physical sensations and exhilaration that come with hobbies like these.

Challenges

There is a bit of a paradox in NN8s' balance of gentleness and power, patience and action, intuiting and planning, all centered in the supreme guide of the body. Body speed is different than head or energy speed. It takes time to process new information and sensations, allow for physical responses, consider the far-reaching ramifications, and make sense of the result. Ultimately, NN8s will move when they are ready, and will be become frustrated when pushed to do so before that moment comes.

That's not to say that NN8s cannot act or course correct quickly. If they are deeply involved in a subject or process, they will be able to draw from their extensive understanding to swiftly and accurately assess the

240

repercussions of change, and react accordingly. However, if the course correction is related to something they have not had a chance to explore deeply, they will prefer not make a move until they understand the consequences to their satisfaction.

Because of this time needed, NN8s can feel unresponsive or resistant to other Natural Numbers. NN8s like to plan, to know what is coming, to be sure all the details have been attended to. Because of the breadth and nuance of their focus, and the amount of work they have already invested, it can be challenging for NN8s to shift gears and redirect. Their momentum better matches that of an ocean liner than a speedboat, and as a small course correction has huge implications in the long term, and they will not make that course correction without knowing where the ship will be headed further down the line.

Combined with the resolve in their facial expression of activation, their power, and the physical sensation of respectful boundaries they emit, some can misunderstand the energetic signature of NN8s. It can be perceived as angry, disappointed, standoffish, grouchy, or similar descriptors when others apply their lens to the NN8 way of being.

In the Real World: Susan and Natural Number 8s

"NN8 enables you to feel your body at a more detailed level than you could imagine. I have had two experiences that transformed my understanding of NN8 and my body.

The first time, I was sitting with a person with Natural Number 4 and one with NN8. We were doing an exercise that included having the person with NN8 put her hand on my leg. She then, through her hand, began to share her body-awareness with me. It felt as if her 8ness was seeping into my body, enlivening all the cells, making the inside of my body dance. I began to feel all the individual parts of my leg – the cells, the veins, the blood pumping through. All of these sensations were brand new to me. This first experience taught me to begin to pay attention to my body at the cellular level. I had never before felt this internal power and ease.

The second time was teaching a workshop about NN8 and I had NN8s sitting on either side of me. I asked them to place their hand on my leg and transfer their bodily awareness into my body. Again, the awareness of the interior of my body began to enliven as their NN8 awareness seeped into my body.

This time, however, I began to experience an incredible body-based joy combined with a deep melancholy. The joy came from the magical power I could feel in my body as I felt into the wisdom contained in the cells and systems of the body as they function together in mysterious ways. The melancholy came from the deep sadness my own body felt from the total lack of awareness that I, and the world around me, have for the power and majesty of the physical body. Perhaps it was also the deep sadness within the two NN8 bodies next to me; indeed, it felt like it was theirs and mine – and the joy and power and the sadness united us in new understanding.

When we share the power of our Natural Number with others, it is transformative. Once it has been perceived and recognized, you can never return to a state where you do not know the power of the other Natural Number. The gift of knowing that I have a body that needs to be taken care of, listened to, honoured, and cherished came through this experience. As a result, I am much less likely to ignore my body's wisdom and much more likely to wait and listen than I was before this powerful experience."

Natural Number 8s Interacting with Other Natural Numbers

Some things for NN8s to remember when with people of other Natural Numbers:

1. Other Natural Numbers are not aware of how important it is to you that they do what they say they are going to do. Others are more willing to make and break commitments. Tell them when something is important to you and why. Don't push others to make commitments when they are not ready, as they will be more likely to disappoint you.

242

2. Trust your body and its judgment. Other Natural Numbers are not as aware of their bodies in comparison with you, but you can share that awareness through your presence. However, when you ignore the information coming from your body, or override your connection to the physical, others will lose touch with their own body wisdom and resilience. Taking care of yourself is part of taking care of others.

3. If you intend to help someone but cannot yet say "yes" to the request, make it clear what you need to move forward. In line with self-care, you must also accept that sometimes you will be unable to help, and that you can allow yourself the boundary of saying "no".

4. Others may not understand that your resistance is a result of not having had enough time to fully process change. Ask for time when you need it.

5. Be open to forgiveness when someone has acknowledged the error of their ways and demonstrated a willingness to change; remember that people can gain integrity through error. When others transgress, be clear about what they did, why it was important to you, and what they can do to make amends. You do not need to forgive or trust them immediately, but remain open to the reality that humans make honest mistakes on a regular basis.

6. The power in the facial expression of activation for NN8s can be misunderstood; others may think you are angry or grouchy. Keep open communication with your friends and family to help them recognize the difference.

7. Remember to let your gentleness be a guide with people. Gentleness is a component of strength, not it's opposite, and you can practice it without compromising yourself and your values.

8. Keep an eye on how and when you hold boundaries. Evaluate their importance regularly, and trust your body's needs. Does it still make sense? Is it the right boundary, in the right place, with the right person? Do you feel safe? Is it helping build safety and trust? Do you really need the protection of the boundary or is it just a habit that has become a hindrance?

9. You know your body better than others around you. Use your strength to stand up for what you know to be needed for your health and wellness.

For People Who Don't Have Natural Number 8

How Others Support Natural Number 8s

Remember that NN8 is about integrity and trust. Showing up in your own integrity is what builds trust for NN8s:

1. If you make a commitment, keep it. If you have to make a change, do so as soon as possible and explain what changed.

2. Sometimes NN8s will meet you with power and resistance. They may be doing so to hold you at a distance because they feel that you are encroaching on one of their boundaries. They may also be checking the level of your commitment, testing your convictions, or, if they are struggling internally, your loyalty. If you meet them with integrity, and show that something is important to you, they will invest themselves in supporting you.

3. Be consistent with who you say that you are. When your sense of self begins to shift, be honest with others and yourself.

4. Remember that all of your actions are checked against an NN8's sense of your personal integrity and trustworthiness. It you do something that breaks the trust, own your part, communicate,

and show that you will not do so again. If you repeatedly make the same transgression or make no attempt to remediate, they may cut ties with you permanently, and it will be extraordinarily hard to rebuild the level of trust needed to restore the relationship.

5. Show discretion when pushing NN8s to action or change. Often, they require time to process the situation, and develop a plan of action – if you do not afford this, they may shut you out. However, when an NN8 is struggling, or has lost their connection to their body, they may already be in such a state of shut down, and need help to regain their motion and momentum. Communicate with them and act on a case-by-case basis.

6. Ask for what you need and give them time to answer. If they say "no", they mean "no". If they say "yes", listen to any thoughts or misgivings they might have about the request.

7. To other Natural Numbers, moving or re-directing NN8s can seem challenging. A small course correction makes a big impact. NN8s plan, and they look far ahead to the completion of a project. They know, through their bodies, what the steps are. Allow them the time and space to make their ideas clear, then work with them to know who is responsible for what component. If the plan needs to be changed, get them involved in changing it.

8. Always do your best. Even when the product may not seem to measure up, it matters more to NN8s that you have tried your hardest, invested time, and put in the effort. They will appreciate your commitment and respect the outcome; this will build trust.

9. You may experience NN8s' power and resistance as disapproval or disappointment. Sometimes it is, and sometimes they are testing you. It is okay to ask. Listen when they answer, and reflect understanding through your actions.

Parenting Natural Number 8s

Saying what you mean and doing what you promise is probably the number one parenting rule for NN8s. There is nothing more disturbing to them than a parent that says they will pick them up at 3pm, and then arrives at 3:30 with no warning, explanation, or apology.

NN8 children love to plan; they love doing the things they have planned. They invest huge energy and attention into developing their ideas and look forward to completing them. They know in their bodies what it takes to do things, so they like to be sure all the resources and time are available to *do it right*. They do not like to be rushed and may resist spontaneous change that they do not have time to integrate. They can become worried if other people are included in and integral to their plan, because, in general, it is their experience that others are not as reliable as themselves, which puts the execution of the plan at risk. This can cause anxiety and stress that shows up in their bodies.

Give as much notice as you can for changes in direction, wherever they occur. As mentioned earlier, it is more like redirecting a battleship than a small boat. What seem like little course corrections to you feel larger to the NN8. They are in it for the long haul, and seemingly minor alterations can wreak havoc with their sense of repercussions. Think of railroad tracks running parallel to a cliff – if the angle is slightly altered, it will make little difference in the short term, but after several miles may cause the train to run off the edge of the ravine.

Demonstrating your own forethought of such ramifications can be comforting to your child. Contextualize and explain the whole situation of what is changing, why, and how it will realistically manifest. This allows for the child to develop a quicker understanding of the new structure through which they will be experiencing life, and enforces their trust of your judgment. If you make big changes without explanation, that trust will be broken. They need to understand the whole of the context in order to feel grounded, and being grounded is very important to an NN8. To this effect, they can also be impatient for answers and can push to get them, despite making their own decisions at body speed.

NN8 children need clear boundaries and structure in order to feel safe. When boundaries are unclear, the plan is unclear and can change without notice. When boundaries are not observed, they lose trust in their safety. When they lose trust in their safety, they can become very agitated and upset. NN8 kids test the boundaries, especially in physical ways, or when reasons for a boundary have not been stated. They want to know that the rules are set, safe, and stable, such that they can plan within the framework. They might even pick a fight with you or a sibling to test a boundary's strength.

NN8s typically have a few, very good friends, as building the level of trust they are comfortable with takes time. They can function easily as the center of attention, but also enjoy alone time to explore. They can feel a breach of trust or injustice in their bodies. If someone makes fun of them or treats them badly, they feel it physically. They will usually withdraw and cut that person out of their life, not having anything to do with them for a while, and sometimes permanently.

If an NN8 child tells you that they do not want to go with someone, or do something, be curious about the reason, and note the physical behavior that goes along with the resistance. Do not force them into situations in which they feel viscerally unsafe; you may inadvertently teach them not to trust themselves, and their built-in warning systems. Support your NN8 child to build trust in the wisdom they get from their body. Though you, their parents, will often need to decide what is best for them based on your advanced experience with life, you must also teach them to listen to their body's intuition. As they develop confidence with their body wisdom, it will become harder for them to be told what to do, so involve them in your decisions. When you get pushback, be curious about where it is coming from and what they are feeling; listen with your body, not your mind. An NN8 child that feels unsafe, or is otherwise unhappy, will try to communicate this with their body. Through their actions they try to show you the source of their discomfort. Pay attention to their physical actions as you would their words.

When an NN8 child comes at you with big energy when they are upset, disappointed, or worried, it is important to meet this energy with as much love as you can muster in the moment. At some level, they are checking your loyalty, to see how much you care. Some may test this actively and constantly; others will observe and record the results based on more organic situations. A struggling NN8 may be waiting for the people in their life to fail them, and watching for that moment. Whatever the context, meet these tests with integrity, consistency, and equanimity as much as possible. They want you to be reliable and trustworthy. When you are, this allows them to relax.

NN8s love to test themselves – their skills, their minds, and their bodies. For many, their favorite tests are against nature – can I survive in the wild? Can I climb this tree? Can I weather this storm? They have a unique relationship with the outdoors and animals, which they may be drawn to. Often, it can feel to other Natural Numbers as if they value their relationships with their animals over their relationships with people – animals are safer and more reliable, and they love unconditionally. Provide opportunities for your NN8 child to experience nature and animals, to build a relationship with both.

Here is a quote from one young NN8 "My mom always says I was a wood nymph as a kid. I got a toad to follow me home once, so maybe also a witch?"

Physical activity, often in the form of sport, is very important. Using their body helps them develop their relationship with themselves, and others. Get them outside doing physical things – it will help them process their reality.

When is Activating NN8 Useful or Helpful?

For people who learn how to create the activation of NN8 when it is not their Natural Number, there are certain times and applications where it is very useful.

1. When you need to make a decision, and are not sure what to do, or what the next steps are, allowing your body to take the time in NN8 to process the situation is extraordinarily useful.

2. When you need to plan something, bring in NN8, either in your own body or through someone with NN8.

248

3. If something does not feel safe, check in with your body through NN8. Trust what your body tells you; do not disbelieve its wisdom.

4. When spending time with a person of NN8, activating their center will help you maintain integrity with yourself and thereby with them, building trust. You will be more able to receive the wisdom of your body, and allow this body-based knowing to direct your actions.

Exercise to Gain Awareness of Natural Number 8

Find an open space on a wall. Position your back against the wall with your legs bent comfortably, with the sacrum and upper back as flat as possible on the wall, such that the upper body is balanced on the sacrum, supported along the spine, and relaxed in tone. Push your feet into the floor; feel the ground beneath your feet create a powerful triangle with your legs up to your lower back.

As you push your feet into the ground, feel how relaxed and supported your upper body is by the powerful connection to the earth. It is easy to stay in this position, as the ground is supporting the body; the muscles should do little to no work.

Natural Number 8 Checklist:

Physical

1. Have a flat sacrum, with lower body energy and power.

2. Have high body tone, especially in the lower body when activated.

3. Have resolute, ready eyes.

4. Have a set to the jaw, and a relatively round face and head.

5. Experience everything in your body in high detail.

Nonphysical

1. Build trust through experience.

2. Know when things are safe.

3. Are great at planning and creating with integrity.

4. Are supremely powerful and supremely gentle at the same time and know how to use both.

If you identify with Natural Number 8 and would like to verify that this is indeed your Natural Number, visit our website for more information and the next steps on your path: https://bodyof9.com/naturalnumber8

Natural Number 9 (NN9)

Oneness is a natural state of being – you can exclude only yourself. We separate ourselves from others through the thoughts we have. We believe that we are separate. We must drop the barriers and step into oneness.

Physiology

Body Structure

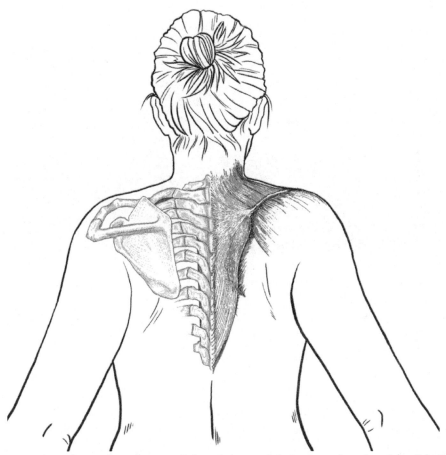

In opening the upper front of the chest and bringing the shoulder blades together, Natural Number 9 (NN9) movement centers around the upper back.

Posture of Activation

In the NN9 posture, the arms come out to the sides and open toward the back. Rotating the palms upward as the arms are brought back opens the shoulders. The shoulder blades rotate back, and flatten along the spine, rolling down and back. In the front of the body, the upper chest opens. Below the clavicle and manubrium, the second and third ribs lift and expand, flattening and widening the upper chest. The body is then balanced around a triangle, with one point at the spine between the shoulder blades at T6/7 and the other two points at the front of the body at the shoulders in the soft tissue between the second and third ribs.

The shoulder blades(scapulae) are pulled together close to the spine at vertebrae T6/T7, dropping and flattening on the back, allowing the shoulders to round out even wider. The action of depression (moving back and down) is done by the lower fibers of the trapezius. The rhomboid muscles are used as stabilizers, retractors and medial (inward) rotators. This forms a cradle along the spine, supporting the scapula, and creating the activation of the NN9.

This open posture is one that NN9s assume when they are using their body to perform challenging actions. The movement initiation point on the back creates a fluid rotation in the body; every movement flows out from that place in a wave. The arms open and move back as balancing wings to the body. If you ask a person with NN9 to roll their shoulders in a figure eight-type movement and allow the movement to extend down into the arms and fingers, it has a beautiful fluidity.

Facial Structure and Expression of Activation

In the facial structure of NN9s, you see a softness in the outside turn of the jawline. The mouth often has a bow-like quality. The eyebrows have a slight rise above the outside corner of the eye.

When the Natural Number is active, the muscles in the face are neutral and relaxed, not expressing any emotion or thought. The eyes also appear neutral, not looking anywhere specific or having any focus. The peripheral vision typically expands, and visual acuity softens.

Some NN9s have a longer and narrower face, but the basic qualities of the eyes, the softness at the cheeks, and the neutrality are all still evident.

The upper chest expresses the activation. NN9s are proportionately broader across the top of the chest with a flatness to the upper chest.

Eye Quality

The eyes of NN9s are neutral and unfocused, and, compared with other Natural Numbers, can look non-responsive. Paradoxically, the more neutral and flat they look, the more aware they are.

The lack of focus, combined with expanded peripheral vision, gives a sense that they are not looking at anything in particular, not focused in or out. When other Natural Numbers look this way, they are usually lost in thought. For NN9s it is the opposite: they are very aware and very present, but their expression does not reflect the wide periphery of information they are absorbing as a more embodied energy might.

Muscular Tone

Most people who embody NN9 have medium tone, and significant fluidity. Often, they can move their arms easily in a flowing, rolling motion, and they can extend their arms very far behind the body compared with other Natural Numbers.

Usually it is easy for NN9s to lay their hands on their back along the spine, palm out, with the back of the hands on the spine between the scapula; even as they age and stiffen, they retain the ability to put their hands behind and on their upper backs.

Gestures and Movement

You will often see NN9s stretch or move by putting their arms back behind their body. They may cross their arms behind their back, grasping the hands and pulling a stretch in the upper chest. They hold their arms out wide, and when they sit, they are most comfortable when their shoulders can roll back and open the front of the chest.

They have tremendous fluidity in their gestures and movement, with the motion rippling through the body to the furthest extremity. They may be slow and smooth or quick and graceful, whatever is needed. Even when they move quickly, they do so without energetic impact on the space.

When they are dancing, you will see the back lead their movement, rolling the shoulders and extending the motion all the way down their arms and out of the fingers. Often, they will move backwards rather than forwards. In performance, you will see them turn and put their back toward the audience as easily and comfortably as they would their front.

NN9s can get stuck when approached with imposing requests. If they get stuck, they will often hold their breath and become very still.

Activation and Its Sensations

To activate NN9 in the body, allow your body to move gently into the physical posture of activation described earlier by using your breath. Breathe audibly, moving your body in synch with your inhales and exhales.

Once your arms are as far back as possible(without forcing the posture), palms facing up, upper chest expanded, and shoulders down and back with scapula together, continue breathing. The awareness expands to take in more, and a feeling of interconnected oneness descends on the body.

The field of vision takes on a one-dimensional quality, where nothing is separate from anything else, where you can sense how any blip in the fabric of humanity will ripple out to affect all. In this space you can know how to move without force, having as little impact with as great a perspective as possible.

Once activated, NN9s can create swift movement and energy with harmony, ease, and flow. To others it can feel as if they are not doing anything; they move and create without disturbing the fabric, at whatever pace is needed. NN9 is additive, but does not change what is happening in the moment; they hold the space without impacting it.

In the Real World: Maree, Natural Number 9 on Feeling Overwhelmed, and Expansion

"I find it easier to write things down when I've had more time to think about the questions. When I speak, I feel I often can't articulate myself very well, and what I say is not exactly what I mean. I can come across quite confusing to others, which I can see from the look on people's faces, and how I feel the energy change.

I wanted to answer a question that was asked in community. At the time, the flow of the conversation changed, and I couldn't think of a way to steer it back without disrupting the energy so I left it and thought I would answer it later.

Someone asked "what happens when NN9s get overwhelmed?"

When I get overwhelmed, it is usually due to me a) taking on too many tasks without acting on the previous tasks, or b) facing some kind of conflict which requires my attention and not knowing how to deal with it without confrontation.

To deal with the first, I have always been a physical list maker, on paper or in my phone – however, visual paper lists are best. I need to make a list in order to create space in the "mental filing cabinet" inside my head, and creating this space allows for integration, which creates clarity in my mind, which is very important for remaining calm. If I don't make lists, I get very overwhelmed.

I haven't quite figured out how to handle the second one.

Physically, what I've noticed when I'm overwhelmed is that I tend to hold my breath, and I grip the muscles in the front of my chest. I am now aware that with this gripping I am subconsciously putting up a psychic guard, which protects and shields me like a coat of armor. This "armor" expands out a few inches into my energetic field.

With awareness, I am now able to focus on my breathing, and I imagine myself pulling apart and opening up this protective armor, knowing that I am safe. This self-protective mechanism is extremely ingrained in my being, and one I will continue to work on.

I often disconnect from the outside and expand my awareness from within – I switch off focusing using my eyes and I go within myself where I use my other senses. The feeling and knowingness and my peripheral expanded inner vision kicks in. When I'm in this part of my NN9ness (i.e. sitting in the background rather than in the center), this energy fills the entirety of my thorax/chest area up to around the level of my eyes and expands outwards from the center, radiating out. My eyes remain soft and the surrounding muscles above the eyes – and actually, the whole of the face – remain relaxed/inactive.

My shoulders naturally sit in a neutral position and don't round forwards. This places my thorax and the visceral organs associated with the thorax (i.e. the heart) in a position open to receiving, which goes hand in hand with me putting up a physical guard in front of my chest when I'm overwhelmed!"

An Exercise to Practice Expansion:

"Sometimes I like to play a game that I made up, which I play with my little niece and nephew. I tune in to my sense of hearing and focus on listening to five things around me all at once. We sit or lie down in a quiet place and tune in to five different sounds in the environment around us; for example, the first sound could be the sound of your own breathing. Focus on that for a moment, then next you can hear maybe the cars on the street and tune in to both that and the breathing for a moment. Then next, for example, you can hear the birds in the trees, and so on, until you can focus on all five sounds at once. It's very calming for both them and me. A very good way to "switch off" being overwhelmed by thoughts and go inside and open up the senses, using the sense of hearing to expand my awareness out into universal space."

Energetic Signature and Focus

When NN9 is active in the body, the energy is expansive. To other Natural Numbers it can feel slow and non-responsive, but NN9s are extraordinarily aware of their universal level surroundings. The expansive nature of the awareness, with themselves as the center, creates a sense of belonging and oneness with all that is, and a sense of one's place in the universe.

From here it takes time to know what needs to be done. Once the fabric of humanity – the tapestry that is this moment in the universe – is understood by the NN9s, they have a sense of what to do, what to include, and where and how to move. But, unless they have time to integrate the whole into their awareness, they may struggle to begin.

There is always space for more to be considered. The focus of NN9s is broader and more inclusive than for other Natural Numbers. When we ask NN9s to cover any topic, they will often respond with questions that reveal more of the whole picture. They do this without judgment; if you haven't told them everything, or haven't thought about everything involved, they will sense this and keep searching. Once they are comfortable that the panorama of the view is complete, a sense of peace descends. Now they can move to action as efficiently as possible, if they so choose.

Values, Skills, Talents, and Challenges

Core Values for Natural Number 9s:

Flow: NN9s understand that we exist in a flow of energy. Their understanding of our oneness in this flow informs them of how to affect the dynamics of a situation.

Balance: NN9s value balance in their environments and relationships. They know when things are not balanced, when one side of the scale is tipped in favor of the other. They are always looking for ways to correct the disparity.

Harmony: NN9s want us all to live in harmony, each person taking responsibility for their own actions for a fairer, more inclusive human experience.

Inclusion: NN9s know when someone or something has been actively excluded. They know that, when there is oneness, nothing can be excluded, so they will work to be sure all is included.

Skills and Talents

NN9s have the ability to allow the neural sensors of the body to expand out beyond physical limits and feel all others in the environment to become a part of the whole. It can feel profoundly beautiful to connect into the oneness with others. NN9s can open unspoken communication between the bodies of those around them – a synergy, a new language of unity.

NN9s have the ability to diffuse a tense or dangerous situation energetically, by bringing people into the eye of the storm where it is calm and still – to a place that is safe even while conflict still rages at the edges. With this initial removal of the tension and charge, the storm can begin to settle, and the problem can be readdressed from a more patient beginning. Conversely, they can create such chaotic storms if they are not in their centered place.

People with NN9 know exactly how much energy to use to repair an out-of-balance flow and keep things moving. They know how to look at the biggest picture and ensure that all that should be included is taken into account before action occurs. They know that every thread in the tapestry of life connects to millions of other threads; tugging on one affects each that it touches.

They are the shepherds, sometimes moving the whole flock, sometimes one specific member, to keep everything moving in the direction that serves the whole. They know when things are in balance, authentically aligned, truthful, and genuine. They hold us accountable for our part in the grand scheme, helping us to see and comprehend our impact.

NN9s also talk about how they move experiences through the life process to completion, by metabolizing the energy in their body and releasing it in a more available form. They help to bring completeness and closure to the transformation process, such that it can start anew.

Challenges

Balancing the flow of universal energy using NN9 takes a tremendous amount of energy when interacting out in the world; they need to take time to integrate, recover, and prepare. When they feel overwhelmed or unsafe, they can construct a conceptual glass box around themselves as protection, separating themselves from the permeating energies. It doesn't have to be a box; it can become a flexible shield to block just one direction. They can, unconsciously or consciously, let the body decide what to take in or not. Though this can be a valuable tool, it limits the potential of what NN9s can experience. To others, it can feel like they have shut out the people around them, putting stress on relationships. A person can sense when they are no longer being actively included or considered, and may become hurt or resentful when this occurs.

Managing the expectations and feelings of others, while respecting their own need to recover, can be challenging for NN9s and those with whom they interact.

In the Real World: Susan Working with Natural Number 9

"One spring, we had a young person with NN9 working with us. Once she settled into our process and understood what we were trying to create, she began to create processes and events to support our direction. In just a few short months, she created a super-clear process and moved our events into place and action. It was almost like magic. When she started, we had a jumbled mess; when she finished, it was clear, flowed beautifully, had a harmony to it that was previously lacking, and made a much wider impact than we were able to create without her.

She actually saw well beyond our vision and began to create a fundraising event that was planned to be inclusive and impactful. Again, she pulled this together with what looked like, from our perspective, relative ease. We had some extenuating circumstances, some information that we had not given her soon enough in the process, that was going to keep us from executing her vision. When we had to stop the flow of the project and shift direction, this was very difficult for her. The direction change stopped her in her tracks, and she had to take several days to recover from the shift. She was clear with us that this would be the case. She told us: "I can't just shift direction and get back to where we were before we started this project. I will need a couple of days to make sense of the change."

This taught us even more about the challenge NN9s have in changing direction, due to the breadth of their perspective and the fact that, when they put something in flow, it wants to continue. If they attach to the flow, then it is challenging to let go and rebuild the new direction – especially without force. Unfortunately for us, the new direction that she created did not include continuing to work for us, but rather refocusing her energy in a direction more in alignment with her personal and academic goals. She was sorely missed when she left, but the impact she made on our process created a permanent shift in how we went about that process and how we understood working with NN9."

Natural Number 9s Interacting with Other Natural Numbers

Some things for NN9s to remember when with people of other Natural Numbers:

1. Other Natural Numbers are not as aware of how wide and expansive your awareness goes. Most other Natural Numbers have a much more defined area of awareness. Natural Number 3s have an almost pinpoint focus in comparison with NN9s; Natural Number 6s are like a small box, filled with what is physically present in the moment, contained within an expansive universal panorama. NN9s live in the panorama. Sometimes it is hard for NN9s to understand the compulsion to action that Natural Number 3s and 6s feel. To NN9s, it can look like they are creating a tempest in a teapot.

2. Oneness is a very elusive concept to non-NN9s; they tend to look at where and how we are separate. Natural Number 1s sometimes talk about oneness, and for them it stems from oneness with Source.

3. Movement, speeds, and energy are used differently by NN9s. They understand how much of each is needed to create the maximum effect without using any force (where force is defined as using more energy than is needed to create a change or shift). This hyper-awareness of what it takes to create gentle flowing movement is only available when NN9 is active. By comparison, most of the other Natural Numbers can feel forceful and inefficient to NN9s.

4. Because NN9s already feel interconnected, their intentions can be confused with the type of connection and engagement created with Natural Numbers 1 through 4. The lack of separation that NN9s feel can cause confusion. Often when they feel connected, other Natural Numbers feel disconnected – because others do not sense into the oneness that NN9 can feel. It is as if the relationship has not been developed enough for the familiarity of

the connection. Bringing in the energies of engagement, honouring, awareness of self, and focus that the first four Natural Numbers offer can be helpful for NN9s to create both a universal and a one-on-one connection.

5. The tendency to strive continually for balance, harmony, and flow can make NN9s uncomfortable with conflict. This can prevent them from experiencing certain meaningful engagements. For example, Natural Numbers 7 and 8 sometimes test rules and boundaries by bringing conflict into the space to see how you respond. A non-response to the invitation to engage can confuse these Natural Numbers.

6. NN9s' neutrality in expression, especially when activated, can be misunderstood as apathy or distance. When communicating directly with others, particularly Natural Numbers 1 through 4, making eye contact and showing emotions or feelings helps them to understand you better.

7. NN9 can be overwhelmed because the change needed to fix a problem is more than an NN9 is comfortable making, appearing too forceful or widely impactful. Remember that it might not be the NN9s responsibility to fix it, but it is their responsibility to raise awareness of the issue. Physical activity can help to re-engage the body's wisdom and get moving again.

For People who don't have Natural Number 9

How Others Support Natural Number 9s

It is very important to remember that people who embody NN9 hold a VERY expansive perspective. The other Natural Numbers do not begin to understand what that means for NN9s to operate.

1. Though you may struggle to comprehend how expansive and intricate their perspective is at a universal level, do not discredit

their view. Your issue, the focus of your experience or desire, is very small compared with the breadth of what they are dealing with.

2. When you make requests of NN9, afford them the time they need to understand how it fits in and affects the universal view.

3. They will understand the breadth and depth of what you are asking more than you do; they will see and think of things that you do not, and they will consider things important that seem irrelevant to you.

4. They may appear frozen, or actually be frozen, when something is too big a shift for them to know where to start. Help engage them in the physical to get them moving again.

5. They may try to stop you or the process you are driving if your methods seem forceful or not-thoroughly considered.

6. Because you are contained within their universal oneness, they know you in a visceral and energetic way, a way in which you do not know them. Be open to their observations about who you are.

7. Beginning something takes a very large effort, because they understand the full breadth of what they are taking on. They will usually only take on things that they believe in and care about.

8. When something does not feel safe, is causing disharmony, disrupting the flow, and cannot be dealt with immediately, NN9s will put up their glass box or wall. If you feel yourself become energetically excluded, do not leap to conclusions; give them time to recover from whatever caused the defenses to rise, and talk honestly with them after the fact.

9. Provide adequate forewarning, and time to digest a situation fully.

10. Try to activate your own Natural 9ness to expand your own view of a situation before assuming you have covered all the bases.

11. Get them involved in a process as early on as possible.

12. Present a reason that they might care deeply about.

13. Bring in connectors to the creation process to be sure the connection is not one-way. If you have Natural Number 5 through 8, involve a person skilled in engagement and connection to help smooth the communication and maintain the synchronization of the flow between you.

14. Realize that if they have energized and are moving something forward, it is extremely important to them. Do not challenge NN9s on a problem or process unless it is vitally important to you.

15. If you have to derail a process or project that a person of NN9 has taken on, understand that it will have implications beyond a simple change in direction. The entire flow will be re-evaluated and something you did not expect will come out.

16. Take NN9s into consideration at all stages of the process; consult with them, rely on them, let them lead, and do not push the process.

17. Be clear in what you are asking and what you expect; make sure they are aligned with your direction and commitment.

18. Be gentle and curious about what is going on when disconnection occurs. Do not push when they are recovering or have retreated. Find a way to be in harmony with where they are.

19. If an approach has worked before, don't expect that it will work again – adapt to the moment.

20. Come with authenticity – be real, and recognize that you are having an impact.

21. Recognize when you have an agenda in wanting to re-establish connection. The less attached in an attempt to bring down the glass box, the more possible it will be.

22. Allow NN9s to complete the integration process before you ask them to come back into action.

23. Remind them to use their body to actively include with gentleness, even when it is uncomfortable; remind them that their perspective is needed.

Parenting Natural Number 9

NN9 kids become extraordinarily uncomfortable when faced with conflict, especially between their parents. Try very hard not to argue directly in front of your NN9 child. The force in the conflict is what particularly disturbs them. If you must engage in conflict in front of your NN9 child, learn non-violent communication methods, and work to remain calm and respectful.

Your NN9 child has an ability to hold all perspectives in any situation. Because they can see all of these perspectives, they have a hard time choosing which to adopt as their own. They will often watch their parents for cues and clues as to which is most important in the situation. Try to be aware of the bodily cues you are sending your NN9 child.

The more your NN9 child is paying attention, the more neutral they look. Their eyes and face become increasingly inexpressive as they expand their perceptions; this can fool others into thinking they are not paying attention. Often, NN9s learn to cultivate an expression more like that of other peers when communicating their interest and attention in a conversation.

Do not volunteer your child for anything without asking them first. They have a much better idea of what it will take to meet the request than you do. Don't make your NN9 child do things that they have not agreed to do.

Generally, your NN9 child will understand the implications of their actions better than their siblings. As a result, they will likely step forward of their own accord to help when they feel they can make a contribution. They may get upset if others don't recognize their impact or join them in helping.

NN9 children can get frozen. This happens when: 1) something is too big for them to understand where to start, 2) they are not truly interested in or excited about it, and 3) the implications of failure are too big for them to handle. When your child freezes, encourage them to breathe. Help them identify the starting point and check to make sure it is something they really want to do.

NN9 children will often identify those that are left out or marginalized in a group setting, and attempt to shepherd the group to include them. They might move the group, or they might move the person, but they will try to do it in a way that has the least impact, specifically on the person who has been left out. They rarely get recognized for their impact, and do appreciate it when someone recognizes their positive impact.

Your NN9 child needs time to integrate their experiences, to rest and digest what has happened. If your child is in the integration stage, let them be until they are ready to move again; check occasionally to make sure they are still breathing and not frozen.

NN9 kids will often withdraw if they are not sure they can add value to what is happening around them. They see so many perspectives that they begin to believe their own isn't valuable. They will wait until the next time something comes up to participate in the discussion. Draw your NN9 child into the conversation gently and help them communicate their perspective; honour how important it is.

NN9 kids can be very sensitive and will often cry when young. They can be very serious about their interest and cares. They get upset at injustice and will step in quickly when they see it happening. If it is happening to them, however, they are less likely to fight for themselves, more likely to withdraw and cut the perpetrator out of their world.

They may adapt their behavior to not draw attention to themselves. "As a kid I learned very quickly how people wanted me to be, act, or behave. I would then comply or blend in to make the situation comfortable, and to build rapport with people. I feel like I can go into different spaces and blend in relatively easily," said a person with NN9 in our community. This can sometimes develop into a preoccupation with what others think, which can again be freezing to them.

When is Activating NN9 Useful or Helpful?

For people of other Natural Numbers who learn how to create the activation of NN9, there are certain times and applications where it is very useful.

1. When you need to calm down and relax your body, NN9 is very useful for restoring fluidity to movement.

2. When you need to speed up, but don't want to impact your surroundings, NN9 enables you to move with more grace and efficiency.

3. Balance and harmony are more achievable when your NN9 is activated. You are less likely to run over others energetically when you have NN9 active.

4. When you are hanging around with a person of NN9, activating their center will help you align your pace, be comfortable in more stillness, be more economical and efficient in your actions, and comprehend your impact.

Exercises to Gain Awareness of Natural Number 9

It is easiest to open the front of the body and practice bringing the scapula flat on your back by standing in a doorway, feet shoulder-width apart; with one hand on each side of the doorway, breathe into the upper chest and allow it to rise and expand. Gently stretch your body forward through the door in harmony with your breath. Bring your scapula together slowly and without force. Allow your focused vision to soften, opening up your peripheral perception as your breath leads you further into the opening.

Natural Number 9 Checklist:

Physical

1. Broad shoulders, with flat openness in the front upper chest across the second and third rib.

2. Arms naturally and easily can go far back behind the body.

3. Fluid movement in synch with the breath starting in the middle of the back between the shoulder blades.

4. Use the breath to expand and create flow.

5. Neutral eyes with good peripheral vision.

6. Softness at the turn/corner of the jaw.

Nonphysical

1. Value efficiency, justice and inclusion.

2. Create harmony and flow.

3. Know that we are all connected.

4. Experience oneness with all that is.

If you identify with Natural Number 9 and would like to verify that this is indeed your Natural Number, visit our website for more information and the next steps on your path: https://bodyof9.com/naturalnumber9

Beyond Identification

Staying Open to Exploring Your Spiritual Nature

As we learn to walk, talk, and interact with people in the world around us, we start to lose the direct channel to spirit that we came with into the world. We are essentially starting from scratch on the human journey. Somewhere around the age of seven we may have our first conscious spiritual opening – that awareness that there is more available to us than is right in-front of our eyes. We begin to wonder who we are, what our purpose is, and what it means to be human. There is evidence that we stay open to explore these questions about our spiritual nature until we reach the age of about twenty-eight. How our spiritual nature is nurtured during this period has a large impact on our openness to it, our trust in it, and our willingness to continue exploring.

We call the decade from twenty-eight to thirty-eight the procreative period where our focus moves off of our self-development into focus on procreation either through creating a family, or work, or a calling. In general, all of our energy goes into creating during this period.

The next opportunity for exploring our spiritual nature comes again after this procreative period has passed. We often come out the other side of this time wondering what happened. Why did we make the choices that created the outcome from this period? Sometimes we have been "successful", other times not. It is quite common for people to emerge from their thirties wanting to make changes to create more meaning in their lives, beyond family and career.

Regardless of where you are in your growth and development, this book is designed to support you moving through to the next level of awareness.

Much of the teaching that we are exposed to today is structured to make us productive members of society, designed to teach us how to fit in, do what we are told or asked, behave properly, and believe in what our parents and culture assert.

Unfortunately, much of this teaching is narrowing and limiting. We experience traumas that damage our confidence. We are misled into thinking that we are not enough, not beautiful, not smart, not of value – we lose our ability to love ourselves, to trust ourselves, and explore beyond what is considered acceptable. Rather than reinforcing the amazing skills, attributes, and gifts that come with our being, our body, we are taught that who we are is somehow deficient.

What Body of 9 has offered to those who explore the activation of all of the Natural Numbers is a return to the understanding of how our physio-spiritual nature is integrated and operates in our bodies. Activating all nine Natural Numbers creates a deeper awareness, a natural relaxation, and allows our souls to lead us forward through our bodies' gifts. It opens us to the potential and possibility for change and new perspectives, integrating the power and strength of the whole being.

If what we have presented here in this book sparks your curiosity, we invite you to explore what is next after reading this book.

The Learning Progression

There is a learning progression involved; as in life, our first exposure to any discipline is followed by study and practice until we reach mastery. There are four growth phases that people experience as they develop mastery in this work.

The four steps in the Body of 9 learning progression are: 1) Understanding Self; 2) Understanding Others; 3) Supporting Others – Mastery Level 1; and 4) Identifying Others – Mastery Level 2.

The learning progression for Body of 9 has its own structure and progression. It is physical, it is nonphysical, and it is energetic. It takes into account the whole body, and as the learning progresses, you grow with each new experience.

276

Learning to activate all 9 Natural Numbers may look intriguing and simple from the outside, but the journey to becoming an expert will challenge all aspects of your being and fully transform you. The reasons you start this journey are not the reasons that will sustain you, and they will not be there in the end. You will encounter many roadblocks and frustrations along the way. At many points, you will be tempted to reject this work and the learning process. It is in these moments that we urge you to sit in the mire and muck until the new path reveals itself. You will encounter many new and uncomfortable states of being, feelings, and learning.

If you allow your ego, your frustration, your shame, fear, and disappointment to guide your actions, you will never learn to activate all of the Natural Numbers in your body, much less become a master. As you move through the learning progression, look for the growth. Look for what blocks it. Do not become attached to the destination at the expense of the process. Mastery comes over time, with learning, practice, and body-based transformation. There will be stages you encounter that others do not. Your body and the practices are the only thing that can move you along the path to wholeness and enriched relationship that you seek. If you stay on the journey through these tough times, and stay open to newness, learning, and growth, then you may become an expert.

You can learn to use your body to expand your capacity to discover, to understand the steps in the progression of physio-spiritual learning and growth. To do this you must find the will to stay on the journey, no matter what is presented, to remember the beauty and magic that comes with this journey to wholeness, happiness, and fulfillment, even when you are stuck in the bleak moments in between.

This learning is not a linear journey; there are steps that can be done in various combinations, but some must occur in sequence. These are the common phases that people progress through. Each person's journey is their own; the speed, depth, and personal experiences within your journey will vary as you progress on your path.

Phase 1 – Understanding Self

- Identify your Natural Number.

- Explore your Natural Number, what it is, and how it is different than your experiences, personality, and behavior.

- Learn to activate your Natural Number at will.

- Learn to use the purpose of your Natural Number to offer the gift of your Natural Number to others.

Phase 2 – Understanding Others

- Learn to activate the other eight Natural Numbers. This is the complicated part of the process, somewhat painstaking and time-consuming, but extraordinarily exciting.

- Include your Understanding of all Body of 9 in the wisdom that you teach and offer. When you can activate all 9 Natural Numbers at will, you have expanded your capacity to learn with your whole body. You are prepared to include Body of 9 in whatever you would like to do next.

Phase 3 – Supporting Others – Mastery Level 1

- Practice the Natural Number activations regularly and consciously – both individually and in combination. Attempt to act or connect from the activated place.

- Learn to activate your Natural Number in others.

- Learn how to recognize that your Natural Number is activated in another.

- Learn to activate the other eight Natural Numbers in others and to know when and how strongly it is active.

Phase 4 – Identifying Others – Mastery Level 2

Learning to identify a person's Natural Number is the most challenging and rewarding part of this work. In our experience to date we have noticed that students need to make their own way through phases 1, 2, and 3 before they are ready to see and learn the skills needed to identify another person's Natural Number accurately. When you see a master at work, it looks effortless. This is true of any discipline and any true master. There is nuance, embodiment, and focused awareness that the beginner does not see and will not understand until they are some way down the path. This level of commitment benefits from having a call from inside to drive you forward.

Getting Identified

The process starts here, with self-identification from reading this book. Which of the nine Natural Number descriptions resonated for you? Which exercises were easy to do and felt right to your body? Once you have self-identified the next step is to attend a Body of 9 Virtual Event. There are a couple of choices in virtual events. We offer Online Identifications to verify that you have self-identified accurately and offer additional learning in community. To find out more about what is available visit our website Bodyof9.com.

After you have been self-identified and then verified, we invite you to explore with us in community. Look for an event near you on our Website. We hope that you will continue to explore your physical nature through gaining a deeper understanding of how your Natural Number informs your body. Having a physical experience of the power of your Natural Number is an important part of the learning and opening to the opportunity for growth. The awakening of your Natural Number in your body initiates a transformation that will begin and continue, regardless of how you focus on the experience. It takes practice to build and consciously use your Natural Number to accelerate this growth. When it is understood and practiced in the community, you can begin to see the differences between life experiences, personality, and Natural Number. This is important in helping you to understand your belief systems, understand others, and truly begin to love and accept yourself at this core level. Our Natural Number describes our most foundational gifts that come with our bodies at birth and stay with us until we die.

To find out more about Identification and Activation visit our website Bodyof9.com/bookinfo

How the 9 Natural Numbers Work Together

This book is a result of our observations of the physiological and energetic attributes of people and their Natural Number. We have also been able to observe relationships between attributes using the numeric value of the Natural Number. In other words, the Natural Number is as important an indicator as a person's physiology. We are aware that correlation is not causation, that just because a certain number has a numeric relationship to another number doesn't necessarily mean a relationship between Natural Number attributes would exist between people having those two Natural Numbers.

Our observations do show, however, that there are direct correlations between Natural Number numbers, and those correlations do predict attributes of related Natural Number numbers.

To this point, the numbers assigned to be *the* number for a Natural Number have meaning. We don't know how, or even if, these relationships were planned. It is quite possible that we have found patterns that are entirely coincidental, but it is also possible that there is conscious thought in the assignment of the numbers. We leave investigation of that topic to the reader.

Nine is a complex and elegant number, as is its sequence. If you look at the numerological possibilities associated with "nine", it is quite fascinating; there are dyads, triads, tetrads, orders, doubling, and other such lenses through which to observe one through nine.

There is a school of thought that numbers or symbols can communicate ideas more easily than words. Within the Natural Numbers, each number describes a particular reality, but there are also relationships within groupings of numbers. Understanding the connections between each grouping allows the prediction of Natural Numbers that will express in a group, based on attributes of other present Natural Numbers.

We are often asked if certain numbers go better together in relationship than others. Each number combination creates a different outcome, and has different strengths and challenges. We have anecdotal evidence that relationships between an odd numbered Natural Number and even numbered Natural Number are 'easier' than between both odd or both even numbered Natural Numbers, although of course any relationship between two people can be fantastic or awful.

From our observations there is evidence that we are attracted to Natural Numbers that are more familiar to us. We postulate that is the reason that people frequently couple with people who share Natural Number with their parents, siblings or powerful mentors.

This subject deserves a book of its own.

Questions for Philosophers

Our data shows us that there are concrete connections between the Natural Numbers that are predictable and understandable when related by the Natural Number. It also shows that there are previously unexpected controls over how new Natural Numbers appear in the world. So far, we have an understanding of what, but we have no idea of how or why this is true.

We stay with the "what" for now because it is visible, definable, and falsifiable. We are looking forward to what future research and experience will reveal. In our bones, we know this information is vitally important. What it means, why it is, and where it came from are the questions left for the philosophers. It will be interesting to see what is revealed.

About the Team

Susan Bennett Fisher

Susan Bennett Fisher has been a student of transformation, seeking to understand and connect with the spiritual nature present in all things. Susan's primary energy, Natural Number 6, was first activated at The Coaches Training Institute's Leadership Program in 2002. It was a moment of awakening that began to give clarity to Susan's life experiences. Once she had experienced her Natural Number, Susan realized that the power within was always available. Embracing this power, she recognized that she had found her life's path. She has continued the study and research into the Body of 9 since that first experience.

Susan Bennet Fisher's background

Susan was born and raised to the age of ten on the eastern seaboard of the United States. In 1970, she moved with her family to Brussels, Belgium, where she attended St John's International School and learned French and German. Through this experience, she was first exposed to international cultures, foods, and belief systems, which broadened her perspective. She travelled extensively with her family and school, visiting India, Kenya, Tanzania, Israel, almost all the countries in Europe, and parts of Russia. This ignited her interest in learning and exploring, which has since driven her forward.

Upon graduating from St John's in 1978, Susan returned to the United States to study Mathematical Economics and Computer Science at Brown University. After a two-year career adventure in financial systems in New York City, Susan was accepted into the inaugural class of the Lauder Institute, a combined MBA/MA offered by the Wharton School and University of Pennsylvania's School of Arts and Sciences. The program was designed to develop business language proficiency and cultural sensitivity in its graduates. From there, Susan pursued a varied career in consulting, marketing, engineering management, operations, and finance – always with a role developing systems to solve business problems.

She met and befriended her husband, Martin Fisher, working in Silicon Valley, California, in 1991. The initial timing for their connection wasn't right. Both had deep personal journeys to go on in the meantime, and they lost connection for 13 years. During this time, Susan continued her career in technology, focusing on the implementation of systems in operations and finance, and she also gave birth to and raised three daughters.

In her late-30s, with her three young daughters, Susan took stock of her life. The path to success that had been laid out to her by her parents and educational institutions no longer held her truth. Susan knew there were many things fundamentally wrong with her marriage. At some level she had always known there was something more available to her than financial and business success. She wanted to be able to raise her children herself and not turn that task over to others or her increasingly sick husband. She knew that she was in very deep, way over her head. Everything had to be changed.

Starting in 2001, Susan joined Al-Anon and began to dig herself out of her co-dependent existence. She began to study to become a Life Coach with The Coaches Training Institute in San Rafael, California. She was encouraged by her coach to begin their Leadership Program. In this program, her Natural Number was identified. The experience broke open the floodgates that had been restricting Susan for most of her life. The rush of energy and power that Susan felt after having her Natural Number identified was physically palpable. She knew that she had found her calling in life. Since that moment, Susan has dedicated her life to learning, understanding, teaching, researching, and speaking about this powerful context for our human experience.

From 2003 until 2012, Susan studied with the couple who had originally noticed the nine physiologies, Alan Sheets and Barbara Tovey of New Equations. The original discovery came from using a combination of their own version of an Enneagram test and Aikido martial arts exercises[9]. Susan took all of their courses, volunteered, and spent as much time in the community of people exploring this discovery as she possibly could.

In 2007, Susan and Martin reconnected. They moved the family to Marin County and continued to support and study with New Equations until 2012, when they realized it was time to begin their own research. Susan had learned to activate all nine Natural Numbers in her body at will. This turned out to be a pre-requisite for being able to take the next step, which was to 1) train herself in the specifics of the physiological activations, 2) learn to Identify accurately. and 3) research the physiological manifestation of the discovery. Susan and Martin have proceeded to do this together under the umbrella of 9 Energies from 2012 to 2020, and from 2020 onward as the Body of 9.

Martin Fisher's Background

Martin Fisher was born and raised outside of London, England. He attended Manchester University where he studied Computation. After following his intuition to move to California in the early 1980s, he began to pursue his career in software and database development. He had a successful career in Silicon Valley where he was an early employee at Oracle, and Yahoo! He also had varying experiences at start-ups around the valley.

At the same time, Martin pursued his passion for learning to fly airplanes. He went all the way from learning on a single engine Cessna to flying Gulfstream jets commercially, attaining his ATP rating. He also learned to fly helicopters. Before he was 50, Martin had knocked most of his material wishes off his bucket list, courtesy of his successful career in Silicon Valley.

Martin often talks about how he went into computing because if needed he could turn off the computer and not have to deal with it. He avoided people because they were a lot of work for him. He didn't really understand his true abilities and purpose. He chose a path where

---

[9] The original observation of the 9 Natural Energies was made by Alan Sheets and Barbara Tovey, of New Equations. The history of their discovery and the direction of their work can be read on their website: newequations.com

he could be successful and achieve according to the conventional definitions.

With the housing and stock market crash in the late 90's, Martin was forced to start again. Despite the success and because of the challenges he faced, Martin realized that he needed to pursue the "more" he had connected into in his youth. He began an exploration into what that meant for him. He explored religion and different philosophies and practices. None of them filled the void or gave him a sense of purpose.

His path led him back to Susan in 2007, with all the building blocks in place for the next phase of his life's journey. Just days into their reuniting, Susan identified Martin's Natural Number in a profound connection that was the spark that initiated their journey together from that point forward.

Susan and Martin's Body of 9 Journey

After several years of getting their children launched, and establishing a new business together in website development, Susan and Martin's life took a turn. In 2012, Susan and Martin started on the part of their journey together that would create 9 Energies, which is now called Body of 9, by attending Burning Man, a 65,000-person festival in the desert, designed to help people explore their edges. At this festival, Susan and Martin offered Natural Number Identification as a gift to anyone who came and asked to know. The gifting culture, combined with the sacred nature of the experience, inspired Susan and Martin to continue to offer the physical identification experience, free of charge, to anyone who asks.

After returning home from Burning Man the first year, Susan and Martin realized that a whole new way of being had opened up for them. Part came from the Burning Man experience, but the truly transformative part was working with the most beautiful part of people – connecting with them in their power through their nature, through the Natural Number Identification process.

Susan and Martin started taking 9 Energies Camp to festivals all over California. They attended Burning Man five times, Lucidity Festival four times, and a myriad of other festivals. From 2012-2015 they worked with as many people as possible. The repetition, the mistakes they made, the process of correction, and the personal growth that both were experiencing kept inviting them to focus their full attention on this work.

Living in California at the time, Susan and Martin realized that they needed to take the work they were doing into a more contained community. Through a series of serendipitous events, they ended up in Bozeman, Montana, where they opened the 9 Energies Research Center. They set up the goal of identifying 80% of Bozeman as a proof of concept that knowing your Natural Number and living in a community where this is consciously known and held in the conversation has a positive impact. They also continued to attend Burning Man and other festivals and gatherings where they could work in volume with people, thereby taking their research into the physiological aspect of this work to the next level.

Bozeman proved to be productive and fertile ground for continuing their development, and their understanding of the 9 Natural Numbers. Susan finished her first book, *9 Energies – Practices for Presence* in 2016. She will re-release this book as *The Beginner's Guide to Your Natural Number* in 2021. Together, she and Martin began to look more carefully and closely at the physiological presentations of the Natural Numbers, and distilled more accurate and specific descriptions of them from their interactions with the people that they were identifying.

Their community began asking for a training curriculum so that they could learn to activate all nine Natural Numbers – and they were asking for more prescriptive and actionable learning, asking, "Why is this important? What do you get out of it? How do I do that?"

In response to these requests, Susan and Martin have developed a comprehensive system that combines online training with in-person seminars designed to teach people about themselves, the other Natural Numbers, and how to activate all of the Natural Numbers in their bodies. Participants can go on and learn to be a teacher or identifier as well, after they learn to activate the Body of 9 at will.

The onset of the Covid-19 Pandemic shut down all of their in-person events, opening an opportunity to complete this book and develop the online Identification process. Now they offer many ways of Identifying a person's Natural Number, starting with this, their second book, about the Body of 9 and the Natural Numbers.

Susan and Martin remain committed to research, development, and distribution of the knowledge and impact that going on this journey of self-discovery and growth offers.

In Summary

You now have all the information you need at your fingertips and it is time to explore. No matter where you are on your personal journey in life, this information will serve you. Step 1 – get identified and use this information to help know yourself. Step 2 – begin to explore yourself in the context of all nine Natural Numbers. Step 3 – use the learning process to transform, grow, and step into your Cosmic Being.

In answering questions such as, "How can you lead the world forward?" and, "What is your gift, and how does it fit in the whole?" you will find a way to live with purpose. It is not neutral to withdraw your energy; it leaves a vacuum. It is hard to know our impact because we never know an existence that doesn't include ourselves and our energy. That may seem silly, but it is vitally important to understanding our impact and our gifts.

If you are ready to be more pro-active and explore with this information, then we would welcome you into our community of people doing just that. We have resources and training programs with information available on our website. You can join our mailing list, download our Body of 9 App, follow our social media, and journey with us to a new way of being at Bodyof9.com/bookinfo.

Acknowledgements From Susan and Martin

We thank the 7000 plus people who have participated in the Identification experience and taught us so much about the Natural Numbers and the context of the Body of 9.

We are also grateful to everyone who helped with the book. We profoundly thank:

- Marjie Thorne, Leyla Kirschner, and Joyce Van Horn for their tireless editing.

- Morten Nygård and Paolo Scoglio for their continued commitment to this work and for their stories and contributions in this book.

- Samantha Kok, Jill Basil and Tonya Lessley for their incredible photography.

- Branson Faustini for all the beautiful graphic design, the logo, the symbols, the drawings.

- The Body of 9 Launch Team: Wendi Gilbert, Paul Gilbert, Alan Kantor, Jamie Hawley, Karoline Rose, Michael Peterson, Meg Treat

- Our review readers, our website testimonials and stories, and all those who gave us permission to use their beautiful faces and experiences to represent this work.

- Our students Jack Schwem, Fern Kishbaugh, Maree Hohaia, and Markus Thorndike. With special thanks to Markus for sitting with Susan most mornings all through covid quarantine online as we wrote our books together.

- The 9 Energies' former Board of Directors: Stasia Owen, Nolita Sweet, Kyla Quintero, Paolo Scoglio, Sandi Davis, and Christina Denny for stewarding this work over the last eight years.

Printed in Great Britain
by Amazon

86873863R00169